THE BASICS

Human Thinking: The Basics provides an essential introduction into how we develop thoughts, the types of reasoning we engage in, and how our thinking can be tailored by subconscious processing.

Beginning with the fundamentals, the book examines the mental processes that shape our thoughts, the trajectory of how thought evolved within the animal kingdom, and the stages of development of thinking throughout childhood. Robertson insightfully explains the effectiveness of political slogans and advertisements in engaging shallow information processing and the effortful, analytical processing required in critical thinking. Delving into fascinating topics such as magical thinking in the form of religion and superstition, fake news, and motivated ignorance, the book explains the discrepancy between reality and our internal mental representations, the influence of semantics on deductive reasoning, and the error-prone, yet adaptive nature of biases.

Containing student-friendly features including end of chapter summaries, demonstrative puzzles, simple figures, and further reading lists, this book will be essential reading for all students of thinking and reasoning.

S. Ian Robertson gained his PhD from the Open University, UK, on 'Problem Solving from Textbook Examples'. He has published work on portable computing as well as articles and books on problem solving. He was the Head of the Department of Psychology at the University of Bedfordshire from 2001 to 2014 when he retired.

THE BASICS

The Basics is a highly successful series of accessible guidebooks which provide an overview of the fundamental principles of a subject area in a jargon-free and undaunting format.

Intended for students approaching a subject for the first time, the books both introduce the essentials of a subject and provide an ideal springboard for further study. With over 50 titles spanning subjects from artificial intelligence (AI) to women's studies, *The Basics* are an ideal starting point for students seeking to understand a subject area.

Each text comes with recommendations for further study and gradually introduces the complexities and nuances within a subject.

For a full list of titles in this series, please visit www.routledge.com/The-Basics/book-series/B

HUMAN THINKING
THE BASICS

S. Ian Robertson

Routledge
Taylor & Francis Group

LONDON AND NEW YORK

First published 2021
by Routledge
2 Park Square, Milton Park, Abingdon, Oxon OX14 4RN

and by Routledge
52 Vanderbilt Avenue, New York, NY 10017

*Routledge is an imprint of the Taylor & Francis Group, an
informa business*

British Library Cataloguing-in-Publication Data
A catalogue record for this book is available from the British
Library

Library of Congress Cataloging-in-Publication Data
A catalog record has been requested for this book

ISBN: 978-0-367-36070-2 (hbk)
ISBN: 978-0-367-36075-7 (pbk)
ISBN: 978-0-429-34365-0 (ebk)

Typeset in Times New Roman
by MPS Limited, Dehradun

CONTENTS

PREFACE

Although we all have experience of it, like other concepts such as consciousness or intelligence, defining thinking is not all that easy. Merriam-Webster dictionary defines it as: 'the action of using one's mind to produce thoughts'. It allows us to interpret the world, solve problems, make decisions, present an opinion, make predictions, and achieve our goals. While we are aware of thinking as a conscious activity, it can also encompass unconscious processes since it is the product of 'mental events' that generate our awareness of both the world around us and of our internal state. It does not take place in a vacuum: we are embedded in a world and the particular environment, including the culture, in which we currently find ourselves dictates the course of our thoughts and actions, influenced in turn by our individual personal experiences, personalities, motivations, prejudices, current goals, and so on. What we have learned about the world, and hence what beliefs we have, plays a major role in how we think and behave. Some types of thinking are fast and immediate – you can recall someone's name without being aware of how you retrieved it from memory, or recognize a dog effortlessly without having to work out what it is. Another type of thinking is slow and deliberate and sometimes effortful, such as analyzing accounts or translating from one language to another. To regard thinking as simply conscious awareness, particularly of what is going on in our heads as we solve problems or reason about the world, is therefore to skip over some important antecedents of this awareness – the wellspring of our thoughts.

This book therefore takes a broad view of what constitutes thinking to include how both conscious and unconscious mental events influence or govern our behaviour. We can consciously decide to do A rather than B, but what underlying processes pushed us to make that particular decision? What, for example, is someone thinking when they put money in a slot machine, or vote for a president, or buy a car? A discussion of human thinking necessarily covers the interplay between two kinds of thinking: the effortful, analytical, sequential, slow kind where we are consciously trying to work something out or think things through; and the spontaneous, automatic, intuitive, fast kind that allows us to get things done without having to spend time on them unnecessarily. At the same time, it can be difficult to balance the positives and negatives that result from different aspects of human thinking. A person can show intelligence and rationality by analyzing data, reaching objectively accurate conclusions, and making predictions. That same person may also show irrational biases or intolerance of other people's views. Where do these differences in thinking come from?

The book is divided into four parts covering different aspects of thinking, although with a degree of overlap. Part 1 provides an overview of what human thinking entails and some of its evolutionary origins. Part 2 looks at thinking as reasoning as we attempt to find a useful or valid solution to a task, real or imaginary, or to analyze an argument. Part 3 looks at those occasions when our thinking is motivated, and sometimes led astray, by biases of different kinds. Part 4 discusses further the motivations behind our cognitions and the role of beliefs and evidence in influencing our thinking.

PART 1

THINKING: WHAT IS IT AND WHERE DOES IT COME FROM?

WHAT IS 'THINKING'?

INTRODUCTION

It is important to realize that the world we live in is 'out there'. Our minds are separated from it and gain knowledge about it through our senses. Shock waves propagate through the air, strike our ears, are recoded into electrical impulses, and passed on into the rest of the brain which interprets them as sounds, words, and music. Parts of the electromagnetic spectrum strike our eyes and various subsystems in the retina convert this light into electrical impulses that get passed on to various centres in the brain generating 'vision' which, in turn, is an interpretation of our surroundings. Other sensors in the skin and deeper in the body detect touch, cold, heat, pain, various tastes, smell, proprioception (the sense of body movement and position such as where your right leg is right now) and others – a great deal more than five. These electrical impulses in the neurons (nerve cells) of the brain and central nervous system generate our internal model of the external world – a virtual reality model. In the words of Deutsch (1997), 'All reasoning, all thinking and all external experience are forms of virtual reality' (p. 121). It has to be a pretty accurate and extremely useful model otherwise you would not be able to navigate through the world and we would not have survived so long as a species. That said, it can differ in some respects from person to person. Some might see a snake and feel fear and flee whereas someone else might recognize the snake as a pet. These are different interpretations of the same stimulus. Furthermore, our senses and our memories can, under certain conditions, be deceptive.

CONSCIOUS VS UNCONSCIOUS THINKING

Human thinking manifests itself in many ways. It's what goes on in our heads when we:

- Try to solve a problem;
- Daydream;
- Plan what to do;
- Make a decision;
- Develop an opinion or belief;
- React to an event or person;
- Categorize something or someone;
- Consider what might have been;
- Learn a complex sequence of behaviours;
- Perform a complex sequence of behaviours without thinking.

That last example might seem self-contradictory but it's there as a reminder that some of our thinking is conscious and some unconscious, and that conscious thought is subject to influences that we are not always aware of. For example, repeating a sequence of actions over and over can lead to *automaticity*. Learning to read is effortful but once learned it becomes automatic. You can't, for example, stop yourself from reading the first word in next sentence. Automatic behaviour, including habits, is very useful as it allows you to engage in a complex sequence of actions without the necessity of thinking about each individual action in the sequence. Thus, you can drive a car while paying attention to the news or make a cup of tea while daydreaming about that nice young man you met the other day. The knowledge gained from habitual or automated sequences of actions such as riding a bike is known as *procedural* knowledge ('knowing how' to do something). Procedural knowledge isn't really correct or incorrect but rather it is more or less useful in attaining a goal. Knowing how to ride a bike or how to find a TV channel can be useful. Procedures also include rules for attaining a goal. For example, a procedural rule might be; 'if the goal is to determine whether someone is female, then check to see if their hair is long'. It might be useful much of the time but that's not guaranteed.

A second way in which our conscious thinking is influenced is through innate pressures. Some of them tend to be reflex actions: blinking when something approaches the eye, babies suckling and grasping objects, and their intuitive knowledge of physics such as the effects of gravity. Other examples of seemingly innate knowledge or automatic responses include smiling, cooperation, child rearing, and the 'four Fs': feeding, fighting, fleeing, and mating. Third, feelings and emotions in general can influence conscious thought including: fatigue, illness, mood, the effects of drugs, stress, fear, excitement, pain, and embarrassment. Finally, you can't think unless you have something to think about – your thoughts have some content. We are influenced not only by the situation we find ourselves in but also by the information stored in our memories. Some of this information is general knowledge ($2 \times 6 = 12$) or *semantic* knowledge and can be contrasted with *episodic* knowledge (I recall sitting in a restaurant in Dubrovnik at this time last year). Episodic knowledge is remembering what you had for breakfast this morning, semantic knowledge is knowing what 'breakfast' means. Together these two constitute what is known as *declarative* knowledge ('knowing that' something is the case). Furthermore, declarative knowledge can be either correct or incorrect. You might 'know that' the earth is flat, but you would be wrong.

Thinking is therefore an interplay between what you perceive to be going on in your immediate environment and the knowledge you have allowing you to predict and

FIGURE 1.1 Chairs: Immediate recognition depends on the culture you are familiar with.

interact with that environment. Recognizing the chair on the left in Figure 1.1 is almost immediate for people brought up in a western culture. However, unless you are familiar with Japan, it might take a little time to recognize the object on the right as a chair.

THINKING HAS ITS LIMITS

Have a look at Box 1.1.

Although I asked you to add 2 + 4, you didn't. You just said '6' because it is over-learned, and the answer is pre-stored in our heads. 2 + 4 triggers the answer 6. This is an example of simple *stimulus-response* learning – you don't know where the answer came from, it just appeared in your consciousness triggered by the stimulus '2 + 4'. You know the answer came from your memory, but you were not aware of the process by which you accessed it. 'It is the result of thinking, not the

BOX 1.1 SIMPLE PROBLEMS

Here are a number of simple problems. Go through each one and try to solve them, while at the same time trying to assess where the information you are using is coming from.

Add 2 + 4
Add 28 + 43
Multiply 43 × 28
Multiply 433 × 288

process of thinking, that appears spontaneously in consciousness' (Miller, 1962, p. 56).

When asked to add 28 and 43, you were probably aware of something going on consciously in your mind. There are various ways in which you could come to an answer but in each of them you would trigger partial answers without obvious calculation (e.g., 2 + 4 and 8 + 3), and then you would have to store those answers temporarily before combining them. You have 2 + 4 in the 'tens column' if you like, giving 6 tens (60) and 8 + 3 gives 11 which you then add to 60 to give 71. Here, you are using the unconsciously accessed information that popped into your head and then consciously manipulating that information. But then again, some of you might have come up with 71 without much conscious thought at all.

The third sum is likely to be more taxing and involves processing the figures and storing several temporary answers or *sub-goals*. For example, one sub-goal might be to find the result of 3 × 8. Another might be to decide the best way to tackle the problem in the first place. There are strategies you might choose from such as attempting long multiplication in your head while trying to keep the results of the sub-goals in mind at the same time. You might try 40 × 28 first, then 3 × 28 and add them, and so on. If it's not the kind of activity you are used to, you may even find that your mind seems to run out of space to complete the calculation.

As for the fourth sum, if you were trying to do it in your

head using the method of long multiplication you learned at school you would be struggling.

The point of that little exercise is that:

- over-learned items or behaviours can come to mind automatically;
- some activities require conscious manipulation of information;
- we need to be able to store information temporarily;
- finally, and perhaps most importantly, our thinking takes place in a kind of workspace known as working memory (WM) and WM has a limited capacity – there's only so much information it can manipulate at any one time, so this kind of thinking is effortful and slow.

Our thinking can also be affected by failing to access the memory we are looking for even though we know we have it (the so-called *tip-of-the-tongue phenomenon*). Or we may access information that is not actually helpful to solve our current problem. When we are sitting an exam, we may remember that the bit of information we need is at the bottom of the left-hand page of the textbook, but we can't remember what it actually says. We had no intention of remembering which part of the page it was on yet that's what has stuck. Context can have a big influence on what we can recall (Godden & Baddeley, 1975).

UNDIRECTED THINKING

Unlike other forms of thinking, daydreaming is not directed towards a goal (although one can daydream intentionally). We all do it. Allowing our mind to wander is easier than concentrating. While it is possible to talk aloud while solving a problem – essentially describing the current active contents of WM – you can't do that with daydreams. You can express what you have *just* thought about but not what you are *currently* thinking as that would disrupt your daydream. When you ask someone 'what are you thinking about?' you are asking them to tell you about the topic they are thinking about, not usually about what goal-directed sequence of mental operations they are currently consciously aware of.

When people are given demanding tasks to do, certain areas of the brain 'light up', particularly in the frontal lobe. At the same time, there appears to be another network of regions in the cortex whose activity reduces when we concentrate on a task. When it is over, and there is nothing further requiring attention, this 'default' network comes back online, hence its name: the *default mode network* (DMN; Raichle & Snyder, 2007). It seems to be able to jump between one mental state to another without much effort and to link to personal episodic memories in particular, allowing us to think about the past and use it to predict the future in the form of daydreams. However, when we concentrate on something, we are using an executive control network that is not so richly connected. To get anything demanding done, the executive control network has to make an effort to submerge the default network. There are therefore these two contrasting types of thinking that appear to be mediated by different brain regions: focussed thinking directed towards a task, and undirected, the kind that takes over when we are trying to get some work done and we find ourselves staring out the window daydreaming instead.

INATTENTIONAL BLINDNESS

A different phenomenon can occur when your attention is closely directed towards some activity, such as trying to keep track of an object in a constantly changing scene. When your attention is engaged in this way, you might not notice something out of the ordinary such as a gorilla walking past beating its chest. Simons and Chabris (1999) asked people to watch a now famous video in which there were three basketball players in black T-shirts and three in white T-shirts. While watching, they were asked to count the number of times the players wearing white shirts passed a ball between them as they moved around and among the players wearing black shirts. Only about half noticed a woman wearing a gorilla suit walking on, beating her chest, and walking off again. The authors referred to this as *inattentional blindness*. Focussing attention can also lead to *change blindness* where people don't notice that some aspect of the scene in front of them has changed or is changing right in front of them. For example, someone might watch a video of a jogger who stops and bends over to tie her shoelaces. She stands back up and continues to run and the viewer is completely unaware that she is now wearing different shorts.

THINKING AS INFORMATION PROCESSING – SOME HISTORICAL BACKGROUND

Thinking involves the manipulation – the processing – of information. To take a very simple example, a woodlouse will walk on its 14 legs until it reaches an obstacle. Using mainly its right legs, it might then turn left and carry on until it reaches another obstacle. Because its right legs are the last ones to move when an obstacle was reached, it's now the turn of the left legs to move to enable it to turn right. By doing this, it ends up zig-zagging in one general direction rather than, say, wandering around in a circle. The woodlouse is using a simple *algorithm*, a rule, that makes use of information from the environment – it can't go any further, so it tries to turn 90 degrees. When it encounters another obstacle, it uses information from motor memory – its right legs moved last time this happened so the left legs move this time.

Human beings obviously have a much, much larger and vastly more complicated structure (our brain) to deal with much more complicated kinds of information processing. However, when we look at the history of the psychological study of thinking and behaviour, the first half of the 20th century was dominated by behaviourist psychology which saw no reason to study actual thinking. Behaviourists were more interested in overt behaviour under specific external circumstances. So, faced with a particular stimulus (S), an organism would produce a specific response (R) (see (a) in Figure 1.2). The likelihood of an organism producing such a response would increase over time through *operant conditioning* (Skinner, 1988) – principally using some sequence of

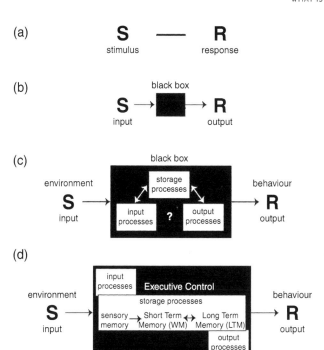

FIGURE 1.2 The development of putative structures in the mind that produce behaviour given a particular external environment.

rewards known as *positive reinforcement*. Skinner used animals such as pigeons and rats in cages where there was either a button or lever that the animal would peck or pull as it moved around the cage, and a pellet of food would appear. The animal would then learn that pecking the button or pulling the lever would produce a food pellet. In these cases, the animals are exhibiting naturally occurring behaviours in that rats can press things and pigeons can peck things, and those naturally occurring behaviours were 'shaped' by the experimenter.

So, what happens when the experimenter outside the cage starts manipulating the availability of food pellets when the pigeon pecks the button? A *fixed-ratio schedule of reinforcement*, such as a one in four ratio, means that the pigeon would be reliably rewarded with a pellet of food only after a certain number of button presses – once every four presses, for example. The reward, the reinforcement, is predictable. A *variable-ratio schedule* of one in four means that the delivery of a pellet is unpredictable. It might be after 2 presses or 6 presses. This turns out to be particularly effective at producing a high rate of responding because the animal doesn't know when it's next going to receive food. It is an example of how a strong habit can be formed that is very hard to modify subsequently as can be seen in the behaviour of people using fixed odds betting terminals and one-armed bandits in pubs, betting shops, and casinos. Furthermore, obtaining food or winning money stimulates the reward centres of the brain and increases levels of one of the brain's chemical messengers, the neurotransmitter dopamine.

While the behaviour of animals in laboratories has been manipulated by experimenters and the behaviour of gamblers is manipulated by betting companies, other forms of behaviour can be reinforced without our necessarily being aware that we are either being manipulated or are manipulating others. For example, a child who is whining or having a tantrum and demanding attention is very likely to get the attention she wants from the harassed parent just to keep her quiet. Thus, the child's behaviour is being reinforced – rewarded – by the parent: in order to get attention, whine. The wily parent can change the child's behaviour, in theory, by ignoring the child during tantrums and then attending to the child when she is quiet. Thereby, the calmness is being rewarded rather than the shouting.

In information processing terms, the stimulus is an input and the response is an output (see (b) in Figure 1.2). This form of *associative learning* is important in producing simple habits and automatic responses to the environment. While behaviourists wanted to ignore the 'hyphen' in Stimulus-Response (S-R) psychology, other psychologists, particularly from the 1950s, argued that there must be something going on – some form of mental events – to mediate between the input and the output. What, then, is going on inside the 'black box' that produces the overt behaviour? A conversation such as:

S: Are you coming to the cinema?
R: Yeah, whatever.

is not readily explicable using S-R psychology. The response, for example, may never have been uttered by the respondent before to that question so it's not a behaviour that has been reinforced. Some other explanation is needed to cover more complex behaviour than S-R psychology can manage, learning one's native language being one example, as Noam Chomsky famously pointed out in a critique of Skinner's book 'Verbal Behavior' (Chomsky, 1959). Not only can people make and respond to utterances they have never heard before, but children manage to learn a language without their utterances being reinforced. For example, when children are trying to express the past tense in English, they learn implicitly that there are rules such as adding '-ed' to a word – 'snowed', 'followed', 'folded'. They often then add '-ed' to words such as 'go' to produce 'goed' which they will not have heard and cannot have been rewarded for uttering.

Part (c) in Figure 1.2 provides a very basic architecture of what must be going on. There needs to be a structure or set of structures that can *decode* the information coming in. If someone is speaking to us in a language we understand, the unbroken stream of sound that gets converted from vibrations to electrical signals in the ear somehow gets parsed into individual words. We also access the meanings of those words as well as the meaning of collections of words in sentences or phrases. In order to do so we must have some kind of memory store of word meanings (a s*emantic code* or *semantic representation*). Along with that there must be some kind of *syntactic code* or representation that determines how words can be combined, and a *pragmatic code* that allows us to understand what the goal of the utterance is. Some examples are shown in Box 1.2.

BOX 1.2 MENTAL REPRESENTATION OF UTTERANCES

Jeff is kneading some dough when there is a knock at the door. 'The door's open,' he shouts. What does he mean?

Ekaterina is in the hallway when her son comes in from the outside bringing with him a cold, wintry blast. 'The door's open!' calls his mother loudly. What does she mean?

Professor Worrell finishes her lecture by saying that the topic is complicated but remember 'My door's always open'. What does she mean?

The sentence 'The door is open' refers to the state of a door when it is a particular position. However, as well as knowing the meaning of the statement we also need to know why it is being uttered (the pragmatics).

'Me, Tarzan'.

We know what the words mean and what the whole phrase means despite it lacking a grammatical structure. We also know that it is meant as an introduction to someone who doesn't know him.

''Twas brillig, and the slithy toves did gyre and gimble in the wabe' (Lewis Carroll, Jabberwocky, 1871)

Here we can tell which words are nouns, which are adjectives, and which are verbs without knowing the meaning of any of the words. This demonstrates the fact that we have a mental syntactic representation of sentence structure.

'Colourless green ideas sleep furiously' (Chomsky, 1957, p. 15).

Chomsky is demonstrating that you can form a grammatically correct sentence with meaningful words but ones that make no sense. You cannot form a meaningful semantic representation of the sentence.

'The hills are alive with the sound of music'.

We seem to be able to accept this sentence as if it meant something even though hills aren't alive and tend to quite quiet places.

Part (d) in Figure 1.2 shows a development of the early information processing models where various stages in the flow of information can be experimentally tested. How long does sensory memory last? How much can we store temporarily in short-term memory (STM)? How is long-term memory (LTM) structured? How is central 'executive' control managed? And so on.

METAPHORS OF THOUGHT

There have been various metaphors, often linked to the technology of the time, that have been used to help us understand the mental events that constitute thinking. For example, Sigmund Freud used a hydraulic model of the mind to understand how repressed thoughts and feelings could manifest themselves in dreams and neurotic behaviours (Freud, 1954). This was like a fluid in a pipe being compressed and hence spurting out somewhere else. An early information processing model saw the mind as an early telephone exchange where input processes were like subscribers ringing the exchange where the operator would connect to the subscriber by plugging a cable into a socket in the exchange and asking what number they wanted. The operator would then connect the subscriber to the number by plugging another cable into another socket. The mind was the telephone operator passing information from input to output. But that doesn't explain how the operator works.

In the second half of the 20th century, computers provided a much richer model of how thinking might work. Instead of having a model that had unexplained gaps such as the telephone exchange model, computers were virtual machines that could perform a variety of different tasks depending on the software installed. Thus, a single machine can be a word processor, a calculator, a designer, a chess player, a movie player, a car driver, and so on. Descartes (1637/1998) regarded a person as a machine animated by an insubstantial soul (a 'ghost in the machine'). By distinguishing software from hardware in a computer, suddenly the ghost and the machine could be combined. Furthermore, a computer works by performing computations. Vision works by computing light intensities; from that – computing lines, edges, curves; from that – computing planes and surface orientations; from that – computing 3D volumes (Marr, 1982). So far, this type of computation involves serial, *bottom-up processing*: the results of one process passes to the next stage that computes an output that passes to the next stage, and so on. However, stored knowledge will kick in to help vision identify what it is looking at and where it is (*top-down processing*). This allows us to process multiple sources of information at the same time thus speeding up the task of identifying objects, understanding speech, flying aeroplanes, or whatever.

MENTAL MODELS OF THE WORLD

Processing information to generate a virtual reality model of the world usually means generating a series of mental representations. If you are planning where to go on holiday then you are generating a number of mental representations about what kind of holidays one you want, what kinds of activities you want to engage in, what kind of weather you are hoping to have, where you want to stay, how much you want to pay, how to get there, the timings involved. If the mental representation is complete, then the virtual reality model you have generated in your head should conform broadly to the actual reality that you will experience in the world, and problems that might arise can be solved before you even start. By mentally representing the world, you can plan your holiday, design a house, prepare what to say at an interview – all before actually going on holiday, building a house or taking part in the interview. We are able to do this because our experience of the world has allowed us to learn what to expect and thus predict the near future. The ability to represent the world is due to the fact that our brains are 'prediction machines' (Clark, 2013; Hinton, 2017a).

RELATIVE VS ABSOLUTE THINKING

There are many examples from decision making to risk taking to perception, and so on, that show that our thinking is relative

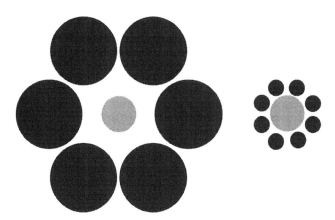

FIGURE 1.3 Effects of judgements of size of the grey circle due to the context. It is small relative to the large black circles and large relative to the small ones. They are, however, identical.

rather than absolute. Figure 1.3 is an example from visual perception. We tend to make local comparisons rather than absolute ones. This is true even at a physiological level. For example, if you have three bowls of water, one hot, one cold and one at room temperature and you put one hand in the hot water and one in the cold water and hold them there for a short while, then take them out and plunge them in the water at room temperature, the hand that was in the cold water will find the room temperature water hot whereas the other hand will find it cold. Relative to the temperature of the water in the first bowl, the perceived temperature in the room-temperature bowl is cold or hot. Similarly, if you are poor, €100 is a lot of money. If you are rich, €100 is pocket money. If you are buying a house, you might offer €305,000 but just to make sure you could up it to €308,000. Another €3,000 is a relatively small fraction of the house price. For any other purchase that you might make, €3,000 is a lot of money.

The ease with which something comes to mind makes it seem relatively important (see Chapter 5). If there is a report of a child dying due to an infection caught at an open farm where animals are handled, parents might think twice about going on an outing to an open farm and choose the beach instead. Thus, the visit to the farm seems relatively more dangerous than driving to the beach. However, such infections are exceptionally rare whereas car accidents are very common.

THE ROLE OF THE ENVIRONMENT

The environment can provide useful information to aid our thinking or generate constraints that limit what we can do. If you are sitting round a table at a meeting, there are several constraints on your behaviour that both the physical and social environment dictate. When travelling, the physical layout of streets or buildings or forests will determine how we get from point A to point B. If you have to get to the train station 10 miles away and you don't drive, don't feel like walking, and you are not on a bus route, then call a taxi. In this case environmental constraints make the decision simpler (see Chapter 3).

The environment can also provide useful information that guides our actions. For example, the redness of strawberries indicates that they are edible. A cave represents a place for shelter for an animal or a human. Whatever we have in the fridge might dictate what we have for dinner. The money we have dictates what kind of car we can afford. We are also surrounded by buildings, machines and technological gadgets that often try to ensure that their use is 'obvious'. The term *affordances* has been used to refer to the perceived use or action that one can perform when presented with an object (Norman, 1988). For example, the handle on a teapot 'affords' picking it up from there. A flat plate at one side of a door 'affords' pushing the door. A bar on a door can be either for pulling or pushing. A light switch affords pressing. In these cases, the objects themselves make clear what action is required without our having to think about it. A door with a bar that has a sign saying 'PUSH' is a badly designed door. I have found myself in a lecture theatre with a bank of light switches that had a set of instructions above it (one of which was incorrect). That is wrong in so many ways. There is also a social and cultural environment that prescribes certain behaviours and proscribes others. Together these influences can determine, at least to some extent, how we think about actions, objects and the behaviour of others. In short, the environment provides a great deal of information that can guide our thinking. Hence, the behaviour of the woodlouse and the human is imposed or strongly influenced by the environment.

FAST VS SLOW THINKING

Much of our behaviour is based on past experience, beliefs or intuitions that constitute rules of thumb known as *heuristics*. We may not be aware of where these have come from, but they will generally produce quick decisions that are normally correct and useful, otherwise this kind of behaviour would not have evolved. Such 'fast and frugal' thinking generally governs much of our daily behaviour. However, we are also capable of careful sequential analysis of decisions or problems we are faced with. This kind of analytical thinking is effortful and can be time consuming. These two types or systems of thinking have given rise to dual-processing theories of reasoning. This has a long history. For example, William James in the 19th century discussed 'associative' and 'true' reasoning, the first being an emotional, intuitive or gut-feeling and the second analytical, explicit and conscious. Here is an example from his book Principles of Psychology from 1890:

> 'Suppose I say, when offered a piece of cloth, "I won't buy that; it looks as if it would fade," meaning merely that something about it suggests the idea of fading to my mind, – my judgment, though possibly correct, is not reasoned, but purely empirical; but, if I can say that into the color there enters a certain dye which I know to be chemically unstable, and that therefore the color will fade, my judgment is reasoned' (James, 1890/1950, p. 341).

More recently these two modes of reasoning have been referred to as System 1 and System 2 (Stanovich & West, 2000) or alternatively Type 1 and Type 2, (Evans, 2010; Evans and Stanovich, 2013). Evans and Stanovich have argued that referring to two systems gives the impression that they are cognitively or neurologically based. They are rather qualitatively distinct types of processing that may be underpinned by several cognitive or neurological systems. For that reason, I will be referring to Type 1 and Type 2 but many authors continue to refer to System 1 and System 2.

According to Daniel Kahneman: 'System 1 operates automatically and quickly, with little or no effort and no sense of voluntary control. System 2 allocates attention to the effortful mental activities that demand it, including complex computations. The operations of System 2 are often associated with the subjective experience of agency, choice, and concentration' (Kahneman, 2011, pp. 20–21). In William James' example, the first response to the cloth is an intuitive response generated by Type 1. Decisions made via Type 1 are often heuristic. Such decisions, as James suggests, may well be correct and are very useful in that they allow fast decisions based on what might appear superficial evidence. There are times, though, when such heuristics can bias our reasoning and hence it is useful to have a second system that can override it using a more careful analysis of the situation to reach a more reasoned judgement.

Since Type 1 thinking is fast, frugal, and relatively effortless, we have a tendency to rely on it most of the time. Too much effortful thinking can sometimes be counterproductive if you are trying to get things done. This idea of avoiding the hassle of thinking too much has led to people being referred to, particularly in social psychology, as 'cognitive misers' (Fiske & Taylor, 1991), referring to our tendency to actively avoid using the brain's resources when we can get away with it. Many of the types of thinking discussed in the remainder of this book can be categorized as Type 1 or Type 2.

SUMMARY

Thinking allows us to interact with our environment in ways that allow us to achieve our goals (see Chapter 3). It involves a mental representation of what the outside world is like – a virtual reality model. These representations are the result of mental processes some of which are fast, automatic and unconscious and some of which are slow, deliberative and conscious. They are generated by the nature of our immediate environment as well as our previously learned knowledge in LTM. Some of this knowledge is semantic – we know about things, concrete or abstract, and their relationship to other things – and some is episodic – we have memories of events. Together, these form declarative knowledge which may be correct or incorrect. We also know how to do things – procedural knowledge.

As well as LTM we have a short-term WM which includes a form of executive control over the information from the environment and from LTM. It is limited in its capacity such that we can store and manipulate only so much information at a time.

There have been several metaphors concerning the nature of mental processes. The current one is a computer one – an information processing system. Information coming into the system goes through a sequence of processing stages in a 'bottom-up' direction. Information already in LTM allows us to make sense of the incoming information in a 'top-down' direction.

One effect of the environment and the way we process information is to cause us to frequently make relative judgements rather than absolute ones. We also make use of aspects of the environment that appear salient and act as 'affordances'.

Modern cognitive psychology has developed from a number of sources in the 20th century including behaviourism and the newer sciences of computer science and neuroscience (amongst others).

It is a long held view that there are two types of thinking and reasoning giving rise to dual-processing theories. Type 1 involves a type of reasoning and decision-making that is quick, intuitive and heuristic-based. Type 2 is slow, effortful and analytical. While both make use of WM resources, Type 2 is more demanding.

SUGGESTED FURTHER READING

Eysenck and Keane's very comprehensive textbook on cognitive psychology covers much of the content in this chapter. The two volumes edited by Holyoak and Morrison provide in-depth background to some of the topics here and in the rest of the book.

Eysenck, M. W., & Keane, M. T. (2015). *Cognitive psychology: A student's handbook* (7th ed.). London, UK: Psychology Press.

Holyoak, K. J., & Morrison, R. G. (Eds.). (2005). *The Cambridge handbook of thinking and reasoning*. Cambridge, UK: Cambridge University Press.

Holyoak, K. J., & Morrison, R. G. (Eds.). (2012). *The Oxford handbook of thinking and reasoning*. Oxford, UK: Oxford University Press.

EVOLUTION OF THINKING

INTRODUCTION

Our ability to think didn't suddenly materialize out of no-where, so where did it come from? Like other types of behaviour, it evolved, and so we should be able to find evidence in the animal kingdom for some of those cognitive abilities we perhaps think of as distinctly human. We are not, for example, the only animals capable of representing the world. There is evidence that others are capable of planning a sequence of actions, making decisions, fashioning tools, and showing curiosity. However, where animals have their own behavioural specialities such as nest building, pack hunting, migrating, and so on, humans' speciality is thinking. We are just better at it; usually.

Toates (2006) has argued that some cognitive processes in animals can be seen as precursors to those of humans. He refers to two types of processing as 'stimulus-based' and 'higher-order' with the former reflecting implicit processes 'triggered by raw stimulus input'. 'Higher-order' processes are an evolutionary add-on to this stimulus-based processing and exploit explicit declarative memory. Rather than relying on stimulus input, some animals reach a 'certain level of complexity [where] goals arise as part of the higher-order computation' (p. 80) and have some degree of autonomous control over stimulus inputs. Thus, one can see the development of Type 2 processing from a basic Type 1 base.

Other than a general higher-order processing, is there something about human thinking that makes us stand out from other animals, particularly those that live in social groups? Like many other animals, our offspring learn by imitating others. However, through the use of language, we can teach our offspring about our culture, our environment, life in our community, the past, the future, and abstract ideas. As we shall see in subsequent chapters, some of the ways we think as adults are an extension of the ways thinking develops in children. Chimpanzees, wolves, and so on engage in co-operative hunting behaviour, but language allows us to engage in cooperative activities that are far more complex such as building power stations, palaces, large Hadron colliders, or mounting international rescue operations after earthquakes. Other social animals communicate as well. Chimps communicate using a variety of vocalizations, facial expressions, and a range of gestures – Hobaiter and Byrne (2014) list 66 gestures they use for communications. Koko the gorilla who was taught American Sign Language in the 1970s and 1980s and showed a capacity to manipulate symbols such as creating new compound words from words she already knew. For example, she spontaneously combined the sign for 'water' with the sign for 'fruit' to ask for a watermelon. She also adopted pet kittens and gave names to them (Patterson & Matevia, 2001).

Another aspect of human thinking that may have been important in the evolution of thought is the ability to infer the mental states of other people, known as *theory of mind*. Again, a rudimentary theory of mind can be seen in other animals showing evidence of being able to think about what others are feeling or thinking (usually *conspecifics* – members of their own species). Many animals can recognize the emotions displayed by other animals of the same species and act or react accordingly. There is also evidence that some animals can learn to distinguish the emotional expression of *heterospecifics* (members of a different species – typically human). For example, pet dogs can evaluate expressions on human faces such as a threatening countenance, although their reactions to humans are different from their reactions to the threatening faces of other dogs (Muller, Schmitt, Barber, & Huber, 2015; Somppi, Tornqvist, Kujala, Hanninen, Krause, & Vainio, 2016). Even crows appear to have a nascent theory of mind since they seem to be able to infer what other crows can see (Bugnyar, Reber, & Buckner, 2016).

Chimpanzees are much closer to us on the evolutionary tree than crows and clearly exhibit a theory of mind. Buttelmann, Carpenter, Call, and Tomasello (2007) conducted a number of experiments on human-raised chimpanzees to see if they could infer the *intention* of a human performing an action. An experimenter demonstrated to some chimps how to operate an apparatus by pressing a large switch by hand which had the effect of producing a sound or turning on a light. The chimps were then given a chance to perform the same action, which they did also using their hands. They then saw the experimenter in one of two conditions: either he carried a heavy bucket in both hands and used his foot to press the switch, or he held both empty hands in front of him as if holding an imaginary bucket and used his foot to press the switch. In the first case, the man was constrained by holding the heavy bucket; in the second, there was no such physical constraint. When the chimps saw the man using his foot while carrying a load and were then given a chance to press the switch, they used their hand as usual. When they saw him press the switch with his foot without any constraint, they tended to copy him and also used a foot to press the switch.

> 'If we interpret this experiment the way it is interpreted for human infants, the conclusion is that the chimpanzees understood not only what the experimenter was trying to do (his goal) but also why he was doing it in the way he was doing it – the rationality behind the choice of the plan of action toward the goal' (Call & Tomasello, 2008, p. 188).

Towards the end of their study, Buttelman et al. state:

> 'it is likely that the human ability to understand the rationality of action has significant evolutionary roots, at least as deep as the great apes. This raises the question of what enables humans to go even further in understanding the complex mental states of others – not just their goals and intentions, but also their beliefs and false beliefs – and to participate with others in collaborative activities involving shared goals and intentions – which, apparently, great apes do not do' (Buttelmann et al., 2007, p. F38).

THE EVOLVING BRAIN

Human beings' ability to represent the world is far superior to that of our nearest evolutionary cousins, so much so as to make it qualitatively different. We can even generate mental representations of things that do not exist. The computer I am typing this on did not exist *before* people could think about such things. We can give voice to our internal mental representations and thereby share them with others and re-represent them externally as written text or imagery. How did this qualitative difference form other animals come about?

Natural selection solves the problems the physical, social, pathological, and geographical environment throws at organisms by adapting them to that environment given time. For human beings, such environmental pressures caused us to be very clever compared to other animals, and this is demonstrated by the size and organization of the human brain (we may have been very lucky since there appears to have been a bottleneck in the human population around 75,000 years ago when it shrunk to fewer than 10,000 individuals). Generally speaking, the brain size of mammals tends to increase with increasing body size. The brain to body ratio is known as *encephalization*. It is well known that the brain size of our evolutionary cousins, the Neanderthals, was larger than that of humans but the encephalization was about the same. Bigger bodies need more brain capacity to control their bigger bodies, although it's not a neat straight line correlation. Nevertheless, the bigger the brain, the greater the complexity of cognitive tasks the animal can do. Over the course of human evolution, brain size has increased some 350% with the most recently evolved structure in the brain being the neo-cortex. This structure covering the surface of the brain is so densely packed that it has many folds so that it can fit itself inside the skull. The ability to think is related not only to the size but also the organization of the brain, although this is not always neatly captured by encephalization. A more accurate way of assessing the relation between brain size and body size is to use a measure called *encephalization quotient* (EQ). For mammals the mean EQ is about 1 with primates scoring above that and insectivores and herbivores below it. The EQ of humans is 7.6 ± 0.2. The nearest mammal is the dolphin (5.3) followed by the chimpanzees (2.4), so dolphins are quite smart too.

However, increasing human brain size might not be the whole story. Seymour, Bosiocic, and Snelling (2016) found that, not only did brain size increase, but blood flow rate (*perfusion*) to the brain increased over the course of evolution by 600%. They argue that this high cerebral metabolic rate in humans is associated with increasing energetic connections between neurons (as high as ten times that of other cells in the body) which, in turn, has helped promote the evolution of human cognitive ability. For humans, therefore, thinking is demanding in terms of its energy requirements since the brain along with the liver and heart generates the most heat in the body at rest. Apart from the energy requirements, there are other costs related to the development of human intelligence and big brains.

THE COSTS OF THINKING

One obvious cost for human beings of being really clever is their utter helplessness when they are born. They spend a very long time learning but at the cost of being very vulnerable. This, in turn, requires the expenditure of significant resources from the parents. An extended childhood co-evolved along with strengthening feelings of attachment and bonding both between parents and offspring but also between mates. However, the benefits to the species of a big brain must surely outweigh the costs, as can be seen by the fact that we have spread across the entire planet and into a variety of often extreme environments. Our numbers have increased steadily since the Pleistocene and rocketed up after the depredations of the Black Death. However, evolution has never been too concerned about some of the costs so long as the genes survive to reproduce. As well as the costs in terms of the pain involved in human childbirth, there was the attrition rate – deaths during childbirth. In the USA in 2015, the sixth most common cause of death among women aged 24–35 was due to complications in childbirth (https://www.cdc.gov/women/lcod/2015/all-females/index.htm). In the 17th century, one woman died for every 40 births, so evolution must have had a really very good reason for this attrition rate (Schwartz, 2011).

This state of affairs was not helped by cultural changes. For millennia, the people with the expertise concerning the problems of childbirth were midwives. Over the years, deaths in childbirth in the West reduced until the end of the 19th century when male doctors began to take over from midwives (there were no female doctors). As a result, deaths in childbirth increased due to infections known as puerperal fever. It has been argued that this was because male doctors were physically moving from diseased patients or from dissecting corpses to women giving birth. Evidence for this came from the fact that, although poor people were more likely to die early than the rich, more rich women were dying at childbirth than poor women because they could afford the doctors whereas the poor continued to rely on midwives. Furthermore, women giving birth in hospitals, where there were both male doctors and diseases, were more likely to die than those giving birth at home (Helmuth, 2013).

BIOLOGICALLY PRIMARY VS BIOLOGICALLY SECONDARY THINKING

The environment has shaped not only our capacity to think but also the ways in which we do so. Our early environment was

not one in which there were cars, civil servants, books, mega-
cities, IT technicians, zoos, and so on. As with other animals,
survival of the fittest for humans meant developing quick intuitive responses to typical situations in the physical and social
world throughout the Pleistocene (from about 2.5 million to
12,000 years ago). A strong feeling of belonging to a social
group (family, clan, or tribe) sat, and still sits, alongside a
feeling of distrust of others that do not belong to our in-group.
Evolutionary pressures and experience produced fast, automatic, intuitive, generally nonverbal, often 'biased' thinking.
The thinking produced by such pressures has been termed
'biologically primary' (Geary, 2005). These are typical of descriptions of Type 1 processes that evolved early (Evans &
Stanovich, 2013) and include what can be termed 'folk physics',
'folk biology', and 'folk psychology'.

Alongside Type 1, Type 2 thinking evolved relatively recently, is uniquely human, and is linked to language. An ex-
panded LTM and WM gave us the ability to analyze situations,
problems, and abstract concepts in some depth despite the
time-consuming and effortful nature of this type of thinking.
Type 2 is often required to cope with biologically secondary
domains such as statistics, astronomy, quantum mechanics,
and so on – the cultural inventions of human beings.

FOLK PHYSICS

While we are born with an innate grasp of basic physics, we
continue to interact with and learn about the physical world. If
we roll something along the ground, it will eventually come to
a stop due to friction. We expect an event to happen either
before, after or at the same time as another event. However,
Einstein's special theory of relativity showed that this is not
always the case and quantum mechanics offends our sense of
how the world ought to work. Our 'folk physics' can impair
our understanding of some important aspects of the physical
world such as those discussed in the section on naive physics
in Chapter 8.

FOLK BIOLOGY

Newborn babies have the innate ability to look at faces, particularly the eyes of carers, and seem 'prepared' to distinguish between people on the basis of their faces (Johnson & Morton, 1991). Children appear to categorize living things as if they had an underlying essence that makes, say, a dog a dog. Very young children have a belief in animism where not just living things but inanimate objects, particularly ones that move such as the sun or cars, are assumed to be alive. Now, one might argue that children have a different conception of what alive means from that of adults who know more about biological entities, but that doesn't account for the fact that many adults for many thousands of years have endowed the sun with some kind of animistic spirit (see Chapter 10). There has been Helios and Apollo in Greek mythology, Ra in Egyptian mythology, Inti in Incan mythology, Amaterasu in Japanese mythology, and so on. Wikipedia lists 96 sun deities from all round the world. Some fears and phobias are biologically primary in that we have evolved a fear of certain animals or situations such as spiders, snakes or heights. Some could be construed as biologically secondary and refer to fears we have learned such as coulrophobia (fear of clowns) or turophobia (fear of cheese).

FOLK PSYCHOLOGY

Folk psychology reflects the fact that humans have evolved to engage in and cope with complex social interactions with a limited number of others. We are good at ascribing intentions and motivations based on variations in non-verbal behaviour, dominance hierarchies, and the detection of emotions particularly anger and fear, and it would appear that there are evolved mechanisms in children to process information about other people. That is, we are born with a theory of mind (see Baron-Cohen, 1991).

Another aspect of folk psychology relates to folk economics. We have particular intuitive mental models of tariffs, prices, immigration, welfare, and unemployment which are often unfounded and make the job of governments difficult. Boyer and Petersen (2017) have argued that the ways we think about economics and economic policy are based on the kind of social environments in which our cognitive mechanisms evolved:

'We argue that many folk-views on the economy are strongly influenced by the operation of non-conscious inference systems that were shaped by natural selection during our unique evolutionary history, to provide intuitive solutions to such recurrent adaptive problems as maintaining fairness in exchange, cultivating reiterated social interaction, building efficient and stable coalitions, or adjudicating issues of ownership, all within small-scale groups of foragers' (Boyer & Petersen, 2017, p. 3).

In modern, complex society, such intuitive views on issues such as tariffs and immigration can be counterproductive, as can being uncomfortable interacting with people different from us.

MALE VS FEMALE FOLK PSYCHOLOGY

We can see the impact of folk psychology in the different re-actions of males and females in certain situations. Geary (2015), for example, argues that there are evolved differences in the ways in which girls and women respond to subtle variations in the non-verbal behaviour of others more effectively than boys and men who, on the contrary, are more primed to detect anger in other males. Confer et al. (2010) give examples of male-female differences in the expression of jealousy from an evolutionary biological perspective. For example, there is an argument that an adaptive problem for men is paternity un-certainty, hence men's jealousy would focus on sexual fidelity. A man would not want to invest resources in another man's offspring. Since, from an evolutionary perspective, bringing up a helpless human baby requires a lot of time and resources to ensure its survival, a woman requires her mate's help in en-suring that this can happen. A woman's jealousy is, therefore, focussed on emotional fidelity, since there is a danger of the man falling in love with another woman and hence taking away resources and commitment to the offspring. Confer et al. argue that jealousy is not a rational response to certain situations:

> 'Consider a man coming home from work early and discovering his wife in bed with another man. This circumstance typically leads to immediate jealousy, rage, violence, and sometimes murder [...] Are men pausing to rationally deliberate over whether this act jeopardizes their paternity in future offspring and ultimate reproductive fitness, and then becoming enraged as a consequence of this rational deliberation?' (Confer et al., 2010, p. 115).

Confer et al. also point out that, if the wife or partner is using some form of contraception, then this should 'short-circuit' any rational reason for sexual jealousy. In short, some adaptive pressures still obtain even when the original environmental pressures have now gone, and those pressures can readily override Type 2 thinking.

BIOLOGICALLY SECONDARY THINKING

When it comes to thinking in biologically primary domains of knowledge, the pressures on our WM are usually not that great as we have evolved to cope with the natural environment using pre-packaged behaviour patterns. Geary (2005) has argued that there is a degree of modularity in the brain and that humans have a capacity (a module) to deal with culturally important biologically secondary information evolution did not specifically prepare us for, and this takes more mental effort. On some early computers, all that appeared on the screen was a green cursor on a 'command line'. People had to learn what to type, including the relevant language and syntax, to get the computer to respond. Other computers relied instead on our perceptual abilities, so that there were icons that represented objects we were familiar with (files, folders, a waste basket, and so on); in other words, we could rely on our evolved perceptual processes and ability to manipulate symbols. However, many things that are effortful to begin with, such as learning another language or learning to read, can eventually become effortless and automatic. Indeed: 'It is a profoundly erroneous truism that we should cultivate the habit of thinking of what we are doing. The precise opposite is the case. Civilization advances by extending the number of important operations which we can perform without thinking about them' (Whitehead, 1911/1948, p. 41).

OPTIMAL VS SUBOPTIMAL EVOLUTIONARY PRESSURES

There are different views on how to categorize the ways our thinking has evolved. The optimistic view is that we have evolved cognitive systems that can make excellent use of the information in the environment with relatively little effort. We can usually make very reasonable inferences based on a paucity of information. A less optimistic view is that evolution works by tweaking what is already there and so is rather haphazard, and potentially suboptimal, just so long as we survive. For example, we have evolved to cope with immediate problems rather than distant ones. If we need wood to build things right now, then we chop down trees and keep doing so until we notice there are hardly any trees left. Hence, we undervalue future rewards compared to more immediate ones even when the future ones are greater (Green & Myerson, 2004). We drive our cars because climate catastrophe is seen as a distant threat and hence has little current emotional impact.

On the positive side, Gigerenzer and Todd (1999) have argued that fast and frugal heuristics can be very useful and often more accurate than using complex computations of all available information. Our ability to call upon heuristics when the information we have is scant or degraded they regard as a powerful mechanism. We can make use of only small indicative bits of information to make up for the lack of detail or our lack of knowledge – hence the frugal aspects of heuristics. If a heuristic is adapted to the environment in which it is used, then it is *ecologically rational* to use it. Gigerenzer & Hoffrage (1995) have argued that such problem-solving heuristics and strategies have survival value and are optimal (see also Chapter 5).

Pinker (2018) also takes the optimistic view that Type 1 will see us through the difficulties we currently face. The ideals of the Enlightenment can counteract many of the biases and ways of thinking we have developed. One of the biases is a *negativity bias* where we are predisposed to react more strongly to negative information than to positive information. Due to negativity bias, we can create multiple descriptions of the various torments and tortures in the nine circles of hell, but we find it immensely difficult to describe what heaven might be like. Such a bias was once useful to keep us out of danger by assuming the worst. But this is no longer generally appropriate, depending on circumstances of course (Ito, Larsen, Smith, & Cacioppo, 1998).

THE SWISS ARMY KNIFE VS THE HAND

Another set of contrasting views has to do with whether the human mind has evolved with a set of specialist cognitive capacities, or is more generalist. An analogy that has been used is the Swiss Army Knife which has a set of different tools to perform different functions. This Evolutionary Psychology (EP) view has been promulgated mainly by Cosmides and Tooby (1992, 2011). The term is capitalized to distinguish it from the general topic of evolutionary psychology as it takes a particular view of how human behaviour and thinking have evolved. The human mind, they argue, has evolved a range of specific adaptations to the physical and social environment in which hominids found themselves during the Pleistocene. According to this view, the mind is composed of a large number of domain specific modules. As well as modules that deal with language, aspects of vision, social interaction and so forth, there are also modules responsible for human thinking and reasoning. Cosmides and Tooby (2011) assert that: 'all normal human minds reliably develop a standard collection of reasoning and regulatory circuits that are functionally specialized and, frequently, domain-specific' (p. 3). According to their Principle 4, there are different, specialized 'universal reasoning circuits' to solve different adaptive problems. They take issue with the idea that there is a general purpose, context-free intelligence and regard computational systems underpinning reasoning and learning circuits as essentially instincts.

In contrast to EP, the new thinking (NT) view regards the *hand* as the appropriate metaphor for recently evolved human cognition (Jablonka, 2011). The hand is a general-purpose tool that can be used for a variety of tasks. Our ability to adapt to a very wide range of environments and to engage in scientific, literary, and artistic creation suggests a domain general cognitive system. NT, therefore, rejects the idea of massive modularity and takes a longer view of human evolution since humans had inherited mental and physical structures from before the Pleistocene. Heyes (2003, 2012) discusses the importance of *incremental co-evolution*, particularly social and technical evolution developing together. For example, selection pressures favouring technical skills support the evolution of social skills, in turn, creating a positive feedback loop. She argues that a different type of co-evolution involving both genetics, *epigenetics* (how gene expression is modified through experience during development) and cultural learning, creates the kinds of domain specific circuits we can observe in the brain. Furthermore, the cultural environment can itself create an evolutionary pressure. A typical example is lactose tolerance which evolved in cultures that domesticated livestock.

Another example is that of reading which is not an ability that we have evolved since near universal literacy is very recent. Reading, therefore, must have co-opted circuits that had evolved for different reasons. An area in the left midfusiform gyrus at the junction of the left occipital and temporal lobes in the brain is activated only in the presence of written letters (Dehaene et al., 2010) so it *looks like* one of EP's specific evolved brain circuits. The debate between the hand and the Swiss army knife has still some way to run.

Although we have been discussing the evolutionary underpinnings of human thinking, our behaviour is not entirely governed by them. Culture, upbringing, and the ability to reason can mitigate and control our natural impulses. Our future is not determined by our genetic inheritance: 'We are not restricted to the modes of thought that come with our evolutionary and social inheritance, but – by thinking about thought – we have the ability to develop new and better ways of thinking' (Bayne, 2013).

THE DEVELOPMENT OF THINKING IN CHILDHOOD

According to the Swiss psychologist Jean Piaget, the evolutionary development of thinking can be seen to continue with the cognitive development of the child. The child's thinking is geared towards adapting to the environment she finds herself in, either by trying to match information in the environment to what the child already knows or by adapting what she knows to cope with novel aspects of the environment. Piaget saw the child's behaviour as based on cognitive structures known as *schemas* – learned patterns of action or knowledge. An example can be seen in the behaviour of new-born babies whose sucking behaviour is an *action schema* that gets applied to almost anything that comes near a baby's mouth. This is due to a process he termed *assimilation* where almost any object becomes transformed into something to be sucked and hence part of the sucking schema. If the baby tries to suck something that is unpleasant or painful then the baby will need to re-evaluate the sucking schema as the new object doesn't seem to fit into it. The child will, therefore, either have to modify the schema to cope with the new object or create a new schema. Piaget referred to this process as *accommodation*. The way these two processes of assimilation and accommodation balanced out he termed *equilibration*.

Piaget was interested in the ways in which knowledge developed from neonate to adult (*epistemology*), and saw this as coming about through an interplay between cognitive structures, biology, and environment (Piaget & Inhelder, 1958, 1969). Hence, he regarded himself as a 'genetic epistemologist'. He argued that cognitive development passed through several stages and that intellectual growth was genetically programmed leading to more and more sophisticated forms of thinking. The various stages are shown in Box 2.1.

BOX 2.1 PIAGET'S DEVELOPMENTAL STAGES

Sensorimotor stage: birth to c. two years

In this first stage, babies' thinking is dominated by the influence of their sensations. They are also far more restricted in their movements and in their ability to interact with their immediate environment than other animals. However, the child is learning about the world by increasing interaction with it through sucking, grasping objects, and gazing at objects and faces. This leads to the ability to play with toys since some toys do interesting things when you hit bits of them or shake them. By the end of this stage, the child has learned that objects are permanent – they still exist even if they cannot be seen.

Preoperational stage: c. two years to c. seven years

The main developmental outcome of this stage is the increasing use of language. By the end of the first year in the previous stage, children can generally use one-word utterances to express complex ideas. These are known as *holophrases*. 'Mama' might mean 'where is Mama', 'Mama is over there', 'Mama pay attention to me', and so on. In the preoperational stage, language becomes much more complex and sophisticated as the child develops.

Also, at this stage, children are learning to manipulate mental representations, although this ability is limited at first to the child's own point of view (egocentrism). For example, when playing hide and seek, they might hide their eyes while still in full view – if they can't see, then others can't see either. Certain types of task can be difficult at this stage such as the failure to 'conserve'. When young children in the preoperational stage are shown two rows of marbles (see Figure 2.1) laid out as in row (a) and then the marbles in one row are spaced out as in row (b), they typically say there are now more marbles in row (b) than in row (a). Making mistakes on those problems in everyday life (say, when their brother ends up getting more sweets than they do) eventually creates what Piaget calls *disequilibrium*: something seems to be jarring in their understanding of the world. To adapt to the world the child will have to accommodate or assimilate new information to get back to equilibrium.

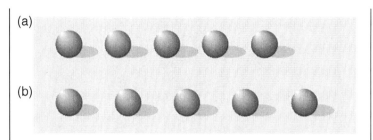

FIGURE 2.1 Preoperational child's perception of conservation. Very young children will typically say there are more marbles in the bottom line than in the top.

Concrete operational stage c. 7 to c. 11 years

In this stage, children understand that certain kinds of transforma-tions do not alter quantities and volumes which are, therefore, conserved despite transformations. They can, therefore, go beyond the surface appearance of things and can classify objects along more than one dimension such as colour and shape. Their grasp of language and symbolic thought along with an increasing ability to manipulate mental representations allow children to think through sequences of actions leading to a goal before (or without) performing them, or to realize that some actions are reversible – if you can add, then you can also subtract.

Formal operational stage c. 12 years to adulthood

During this stage, children become adults both physically and in their modes of thinking. The phrase *formal operations* means the ability to perform logical operations on the contents of a mental representation. That is, the young adult can now engage in abstract thought: philosophizing and hypothesizing. Piaget believed that abstract and formal scientific thinking finally develops since thinking becomes more systematic and strategic.

There is plenty of evidence that children's thinking becomes more sophisticated as they develop but, rather than this being due to biologically predetermined stages, it is more likely to be due to developments such as improved psycho-motor co-ordination, increased knowledge of the world, improved information processing speed and efficiency, and auto-matization – particularly the increasing ease with which children can read (Case, 1985; Halford, 1993). Piaget's de-scription of the stages suggests that nothing much happens in terms of cognitive development after adolescence. However, it is doubtful that a 50 year old sees the world in the same way as a 15 year old. Fortunately. Furthermore, if there are pre-determined stages, then practice isn't going to help as the child will not be 'ready'. However, there has long been evi-dence that practice can make a difference in Piaget's devel-opmental tasks (Baillargeon, 1995; Danner and Day, 1977; Donaldson, 1978). The current information processing view is that many children can demonstrate the abilities Piaget as-cribes to a stage at an earlier age than he thought. For ex-ample, there is evidence that not only can four- and five-year-old children take the visual perspective of someone else looking at a scene, three-year-old children also show that they know how an object looks to someone else from a different perspective. There can also be large individual differences between children in terms of when children reach certain developmental goals such as object permanence or con-servation of number (Field, 1987; Halford, 1982). There can also be differences within children. Egocentrism might be a fleeting event, but conservation might take a while. Other criticisms of Piaget's work include the fact that it was based largely on a small number of children – observations of his own three children (Piaget & Inhelder, 1958, 1969) and those from families of high socioeconomic status. Hence, applying his findings to children in general is not straightforward.

There is also a view that a sizeable minority of adults never reach the stage of formal operations (Gipson, Abraham, & Renner, 1989) while some children get there quite early on. Indeed, very young children are capable of complex deductive inferences in situations that make sense to them. Thornton (1995) presents this example from a child aged about two.

'Child (very aggrieved):   Jack broke my car!
Mother: He didn't...
Child: He did! He did! Harry didn't go there [the playroom] – Jack broke my car!

The interesting point in this accusation is the clear and surprisingly complex chain of inference it involves: if the car is broken, then someone must have done something to break it; if someone broke the car, then they must have been in the playroom (where the car was) at the time. If Jack went into the playroom and Harry didn't, then only Jack could have broken the car, so he is the main suspect' (Thornton, 1995, p. 14).

SUMMARY

Human thinking is a result of a long evolutionary process, and we can see some antecedents of thought in the animal kingdom. These include tool use, predicting intentions, and a rudimentary theory of mind. Environmental pressures increased the capacity of our brains and hence our capacity to deal with complex cognitive tasks. Our ability to represent the world is so far ahead of other apes that it is qualitatively different. A side effect of larger brains is the time it takes to walk, talk, and learn about the world; defenselessness; and difficulties in childbirth.

Because of the kinds of evolutionary pressures, we encountered in small hunter-gatherer groups, certain topics are more natural to us than others. As a result, we have developed a degree of 'folk' wisdom and heuristics covering biology, botany, social interaction, and the physical world. These are 'biologically primary' domains and rely often on Type 1 thinking with Type 2 applied when greater analysis is needed. We also have to adapt the cognitions evolved for biologically primary areas to cope with new 'biologically secondary' domains such as chemistry, ancient history, statistics, and so on.

While heuristics are viewed as necessary, there are differences of emphasis about their usefulness. On one hand, they might lead to irrational behaviour and on the other, they have helped us survive by making use of stable properties of the environment. According to the EP view, we have evolved a set of specialist cognitive capacities represented by the 'Swiss Army Knife' whereas the NT view sees our capacities as the co-evolution of multiple capacities that are not therefore separate and modular and is represented by the metaphor of the 'hand'.

The way we have evolved impacts on the ways children's thinking develops and becomes more sophisticated over time. Piaget proposed a number of stages that children go through to eventually arrive at the stage of 'formal operations' where the child can engage in abstract thought and scientific thinking. More recent Neo-Piagetian views see Piaget's stages as developments and improvements in information processing speed and efficiency that come about through maturation.

As we shall see in later chapters, aspects of thinking deemed childlike can persist into adulthood.

SUGGESTED FURTHER READING

Cosmides, L., & Tooby, J. (2013, 2013/01/03). Evolutionary psychology: New perspectives on cognition and motivation. *Annual Review of Psychology*, *64*(1), 201–229. Retrieved from https://doi.org/10.1146/annurev.psych.121208.131628

Geary, D. C. (2005). *The origin of mind: Evolution of brain, cognition, and general intelligence.* Washington, DC: American Psychological Association.

Heyes, C. (2012). New thinking: The evolution of human cognition [Article]. *Philosophical Transactions of the Royal Society B: Biological Sciences*, *367*(1599), 2091–2096. Retrieved from https://doi.org/10.1098/rstb.2012.0111

PART 2

THINKING AS REASONING

PROBLEM-SOLVING

INTRODUCTION

Almost all of our waking lives we are faced with situations where there is a task we have to accomplish – tasks that range from the mundane and trivial to the noble and perverse. Making a judgement, choosing a dress, solving an equation, and trying to understand an argument are all examples of problems. They can be imposed on us by the nature of our work or at school, or they can be ones we impose on ourselves such as playing sudoku or writing books. Sometimes we know exactly what to do to accomplish the task and sometimes we don't. If you know what to do and can call up a ready-made solution from memory, then your situation is not all that problematic. Your car has a puncture, you need to change the tyre; you've done this many times before, you just get on with it. If you don't immediately know what to do, well then you really do have a problem. If your new car no longer comes with a spare tyre, what are you supposed to do? In such circumstances, you need to engage in thinking. 'What to do' normally involves thinking through a sequence of actions (mental operations), familiar or otherwise, that need to be performed.

These goal-directed sequences of actions constitute what is commonly known as problem-solving. An individual's waking life may be spent dealing with problems from the local ('What shall I wear today?') to the cosmic ('So what exactly is the nature of dark energy?'). These two examples might even be problems that are faced by the same person.

Thinking through a sequence of actions before performing them means working through a series of *knowledge states*. The particular sequence of ideas or states constitutes a mental representation of what might happen in the real world if you perform certain actions. Familiar problems are straightforward but what if the means to solving a new problem do not come readily to mind? For example, how do you loosen a screw when you don't have a screwdriver to hand? Or what do you cook for dinner given the paucity of ingredients in the larder and Gail is a vegan? This kind of problem-solving is more effortful. Fortunately, most of the time we don't have to rely on our limited capacity to think and can rely instead on such useful cognitive mechanisms such as habits, automatic processing, heuristics, and pattern recognition. Routine tasks don't require much thought since we can learn to do them without, well... thinking. Driving to work makes use of actions that are automatic and do not require conscious attention except in unusual circumstances. Sometimes a mental representation is based on experience of solving similar problems in the past so we can apply what we already know to solve the now familiar problem we are faced with. How to lay out a dress pattern on a piece of fabric is easier with experience. Once we have consciously learned certain actions and sequences of actions that apply in specific circumstances, we can delegate them to lower-level processes. We can, if you like, think of the mind as a hierarchy with the boss at the top who performs an executive function and minions who get on with the boring repetitive tasks that allow the system to run smoothly. When a new set of circumstances in the outside world makes itself known, the executive has to take over the detailed running of the system and the whole process slows right down.

BOUNDED RATIONALITY

In his writings about decision-making and problem-solving, Simon (1975) emphasized the importance of both the environment and the information it affords, and the computational limitations of the organism processing the available information. Because of these limits to our cognitive system, Simon referred to our ability to reason as being 'bounded'. Given our *bounded rationality*, we make use of the patterns and regularities in the environment to make sense of and navigate through the world. They allow us to make inferences and predictions that go beyond the information immediately before us. For example, if someone says the dinner was ruined because of a power cut, you can infer that there was food being cooked, that this took place in a kitchen, that the cooking involved electricity, that there was probably no light, and so on.

There are several reasons why a particular problem or task may be hard. The most obvious one is that you know absolutely nothing about the topic of the problem. You can't translate '*Nemo me impune lacessit, Jacobe*' unless you know some Latin. Failing to solve a problem or to understand a situation one is unfamiliar with is not a failure of intelligence, it's a failure of knowledge (Newell, 1990). As in the game show 'Who Wants to Be a Millionaire', the problems are easy when you know the answer. For the same reason some situations or events can be baffling when you find yourself in a different culture as sometimes happens when you go on holiday. Imagine staying in a nice apartment in a quiet residential area in a town in southern Turkey. At four o'clock in the morning, you are awakened by the sound of someone walking down the street banging a drum. What are you going to make of it? Any interpretation will be based on what you are familiar with. Who makes this kind of noise at four in the morning back home? Well, usually no one. Perhaps it's a drunk youth engaged in some anti-social behaviour. So, what do you do? Call the police and hope someone on the phone speaks English? It's a worrying situation to be in. People like to know what's going on. Some time later, you discover that your holiday coincides with Ramadan and that the drummer is performing a public service by waking people up so that they can eat during the hours of darkness since Muslims fast between dawn and dusk. All is now clear because you now have the relevant knowledge.

Another difficulty is that we must have some idea, however vague, of what the goal is in advance. It may be very precise, such as getting a golf ball into a particular hole or it may be vague, such as getting someone in checkmate or world peace. In these cases, you might recognize the goal state when or if you get there but specifying exactly what the chessboard will look like or the exact state of the world in advance is not possible.

WELL-DEFINED AND ILL-DEFINED PROBLEMS

On rare occasions, you might find yourself presented with problems, such as puzzles, that have all the information you need to solve it (except how to do it). In the second half of the last century, puzzles became a useful way to investigate the cognitive processes people used when solving problems. The most influential work at the time was Newell and Simon's 'Human Problem Solving' (Newell & Simon, 1972). Many puzzles are well-defined – you are given all the information needed to go about solving it. Starting with the statement of the problem (the initial state), people are asked to get to a goal state (the state of the problem when you reach a solution). There are things you can do to move through the problem known as operators and things you are not able to do known as operator restrictions. Box 3.1 shows a simple example.

In problems like these, you know exactly where you are at the beginning of the problem and exactly where you want to end up. You are also told what you have to do and what you are not allowed to do. Each time you move a coin, the problem is in a new state. There are many problem states you can reach in this problem, some of which are dead ends. The solution is shown at the end of the chapter (see Figure 3.10). Another important aspect of a problem is the constraints that the problem imposes. Constraints do not necessarily make problems or choices harder –

they can make them a lot easier. Choosing between 3 things is easier than choosing between 20. If you are looking at a menu where all 50 dishes look delicious, you can ignore entire categories if you don't eat meat and don't like fish.

MEANS-ENDS ANALYSIS

Because our rationality is 'bounded', we generally need to break problems down into manageable sub-goals and deal with those one at a time. We are engaged in some kind of *means-ends analysis*; i.e., by means of what sequence of actions and sub-goals can we attain our overall goal? A problem can, therefore, be represented as a 'goal stack' where each sub-goal on the way to the overall goal gets 'popped' from the stack until the overall goal is reached (Anderson, 1993; Anderson & Lebiere, 1998; Hodgetts & Jones, 2006). Making a nice pie for dinner involves a number of sub-goals such as making the

BOX 3.1 THE EIGHT COINS PROBLEM

Initial state: Starting with an arrangement of coins above (Figure 3.1),
   Operator: Move coins so you end up in the goal state.
   Restrictions: A coin can only move to an empty space adjacent to it and can jump over only ONE coin of either colour. Silver coins can only move to the right and copper coins to the left

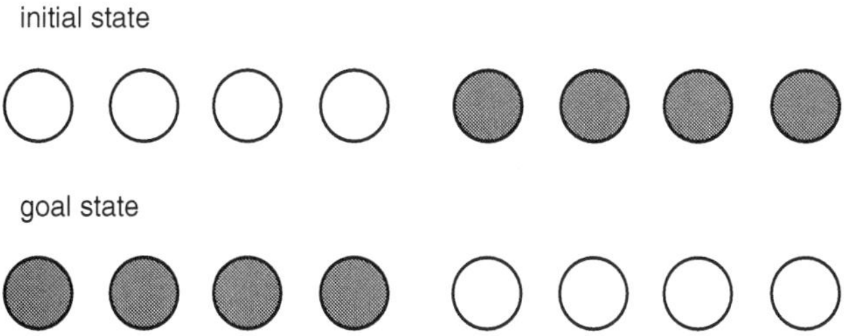

initial state

goal state

FIGURE 3.1 The Eight Coins problem.

pastry, preparing the ingredients, putting them in the pie dish, putting the pie dish in the oven, and switching it on. At the end of an hour or so, the pie is ready, and you take it out of the oven. The overall goal is achieved. Bear in mind, though, that there is no guarantee the action we think of to achieve each sub-goal is the best one under the circumstances. Not only that but you've left the oven on. That wasn't specified as one of the sub-goals since it has to happen after the main goal is achieved.

All the possible intermediate states a problem can get into on the way to the solution, along with the initial state and the goal state, is known as the *problem space* (Newell 1972). Figure 3.2 shows the initial state and goal state of the three-ring version of the Towers of Hanoi (ToH) puzzle. The goal is to move the rings from the leftmost peg to the rightmost peg. The restrictions are that you can move only one ring at a time and that you cannot put a larger ring on a smaller one. In order to move the large ring onto the rightmost peg you need to get the other two rings out of the way. Solving the two-ring problem first is, therefore, a sub-goal.

The full state space for the three ring ToH is shown in Figure 3.3.

Figure 3.3 represents an omniscient psychologist's view of whole of the ToH problem space. Armed with this information, the psychologist can examine the behaviour of human beings and compare their behaviour with the idealized behaviour needed to move from the initial state at the top to the goal state at the bottom left. Such behaviour will include the path taken through the problem, the patterns of hesitations and pauses indicating thinking, whether they avoid going back to a previous state, the time taken, the number of moves taken, and so on.

The ToH is a relatively simple problem with a simple solution structure. Psychologists are also interested in other much more complex well-defined problems such as chess. Chess also has an initial state – the chessboard and pieces set up at the beginning of the game – and all the rules including what you can do (legal operators) and can't do (restrictions). Unlike the Eight Coins problem or the ToH, however, the goal state is only vaguely specified by a set of criteria rather than by a fixed pattern of pieces. There is a limit to how deeply we can look into a complex

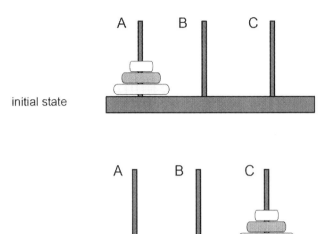

FIGURE 3.2 The three ring Towers of Hanoi Problem. The goal is to move the rings from one peg to another moving only one at a time and not placing a larger ring on a smaller one.

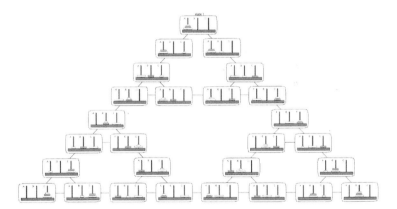

FIGURE 3.3 The space of all the states that can be reached in the three ring ToH from the initial state at the top. Each of the three smaller triangles within the larger one represents the states that can be reached by two rings.

problem such as chess. The rules can be stated in a few paragraphs: they provide you with everything you need to know to play a game except how to win one. But the problem space is huge. A chess player can make a large number of possible moves and the opponent can counter with many more moves, and so on. After only six moves by both players, there are over nine million possible positions they could theoretically end up in. In computational terms, there is a 'combinatorial explosion' of possibilities. The chess playing computer Deep Blue, which won against world champion Garry Kasparov back in 1997, could consider 200 million chess positions per second. People don't have that kind of processing capacity.

THE DEVELOPMENT OF EXPERTISE

Chess is different from the ToH problem in many ways apart from the goal state being only vaguely specified. Chess players can have a wealth of knowledge behind them that doesn't apply to the coins problem including a vast memory for patterns of pieces on the chessboard and relevant strategies in certain circumstances. There is, therefore, no need for the Grand Master to rely entirely on WM nor to assume that a Grand Master's memory is any better than anyone else's (Simon & Chase, 1973). Chess has, therefore, been a useful domain for studying the development of expertise and the nature of expert-novice differences (Chase & Simon, 1973; De Groot, 1965; Gobet, 2016; Gobet & Simon, 1996). Chess expertise comes about through extensive practice (Charness, Krampe, & Mayr, 1996). Expertise can also come about through increasing familiarity with a category of problems in other domains such as mathematics, soap operas, knitting, or whatever. However, learning a new domain has to start somewhere. At the beginning, a novice learner has to be able to transfer learning from an initial example in a textbook or in LTM to another problem of the same type.

Your current problem would be pretty easy to solve if the previous problem was identical to it. Problems of the same type can vary, however, which can give rise to a number of potential difficulties in using an earlier analogue to solve a current problem. Some problems can be fairly similar to the earlier example (the 'exemplar' in Figure 3.4) – these are *close variants* to the exemplar and would probably be easy to solve using the exemplar to derive the solution. The details would be the same, so all you need to do is imitate what was done in the exemplar. *Distant variants* in Figure 3.4 may be either superficially different or structurally different but still similar at an abstract level. For example, many problems relating to speed, currency conversion, electricity consumption are often versions of an underlying simple A = B × C form.

Box 3.2 has two variants of the ToH puzzle.

Both of these problems are variants of the ToH puzzle. Figure 3.5 shows the mapping between the ToH and the Himalayan Tea Ceremony.

While the three ring ToH and the Tea Ceremony take a minimum of seven moves to complete, the Monsters and Globes problem is based on a slightly simpler five move version of the ToH. In Figure 3.6, the height of the pegs represents the size of the monsters and the position of the rings represents the size of the globes. The first move/change is for the large monster to expand the globe to large (represented in the figure by a 'ghost' ring on the large peg in [1]). Then the large globe held by the medium monster can move to the tall peg (represented by the 'ghost' ring on the medium peg [2]). The large globe held by the large monster then shrinks to small again (3) allowing the medium monster to shrink to medium size (4), and so on. (An animation demonstrating the mapping between the monsters and globes and the ToH can be found at http://gocognitive.net/demo/monsters-and-globes-problem.)

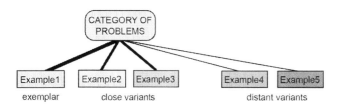

FIGURE 3.4 A range of related problems can form a category.

BOX 3.2 TWO VARIANTS OF THE TOWERS OF HANOI PUZZLE

The Himalayan Tea Ceremony Problem

In the inns of certain Himalayan villages is practised a most civilized and refined tea ceremony. The ceremony involves a host and exactly two guests, neither more nor less. When his guests have arrived and have seated themselves at his table, the host performs three services for them. These services are listed below in the order of the nobility which the Himalayans attribute to them:

stoking the fire,

fanning the flames,

passing the rice cakes.

During the ceremony, any of those present may ask another, "Honoured Sir, may I perform this onerous task for you?"

However, a person may request of another only the least noble of the tasks which the other is performing. Furthermore, if a person is performing any tasks, then he may not request a task which is nobler than the noblest task he is already performing. Custom requires that by the time the tea ceremony is over, all of the tasks will have been transferred from the host to the most senior of his guests.

How may this be accomplished?

(Adapted from Simon & Hayes, 1976, p. 169)

The Monsters and Globes (Change) Problem

Three five-handed extraterrestrial monsters were holding three crystal globes. Because of the quantum-mechanical peculiarities of their neighbourhood, both monsters and globes come in exactly three sizes with no others permitted: small, medium, and large. The medium-sized monster was holding the small globe; the small monster was holding the large globe; and the large monster was holding the medium-sized globe. Since this situation offended their keenly developed sense of symmetry, they proceeded *to shrink and expand the globes* so that each monster would have a globe proportionate to his own size. Monster etiquette complicated the solution of the problem since it requires:

that only one globe may be changed at a time,
that if two globes are of the same size, only the globe held by the larger
monster can be changed, and
that a globe may not be changed by a monster who is holding a larger
globe.

By what sequence of changes could the monsters have solved the problem?

(Hayes & Simon, 1977, p. 24)

In summary, there are several cognitive processes involved in analogical problem solving (see Figure 3.7). First of all, there has to be something about the current problem that reminds you about a previous one and that, therefore, allows you to retrieve a relevant problem (1 in the figure). You then need to identify those elements in the example problem that relate to the one you are trying to solve (2 in the figure). For example, the small ring in the ToH maps to stoking the fires in the Himalayan Tea Ceremony. The solution procedure from the example is applied to the new (test) problem (3) using those mapped features. If the test problem is a more distant variant, then the solution procedure will have to be adapted to a greater or lesser extent (4). Mapping and adapting the ToH problem to the Monsters and Globes problem is tricky and time-consuming. As a result of applying a learned procedure from an example to a new problem, you start to learn something about this category of problems. That is, you can begin to develop a schema for problems of this type that will become more and more abstract with further problem-solving within this category of problems (5).

While it is relatively easy to study puzzle problems such as those, in the real world of everyday problems, studying transfer of learning from one situation or problem to another is more difficult. Lawyers, doctors, and tax inspectors may use a form of analogical problem-solving called case-based reasoning (Jonassen & Hernandez-Serrano, 2002; Kolodner, 1993) where a current case or set of symptoms may remind you of an earlier case which can be adapted to deal with the current one.

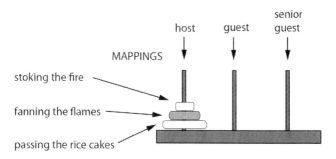

FIGURE 3.5 Mappings between the ToH and the Himalayan Tea Ceremony (Simon & Hayes, 1976).

Transferring what you have learned from one situation to a new one is ubiquitous. For example, in learning a foreign language, a grammatical construction learned in one context has to be applied to new verbs or nouns in another. It is a process of induction through which we learn about mathematics, chemistry, geography, medicine – the world, in short. At the very early stages of learning, it is not uncommon for novices unfamiliar with a domain to simply imitate an example (Robertson, 2000). Only with some familiarity can one start to represent the problem enough to plan ahead. Planning a holiday, for example, involves a mental representation of a sequence of steps often starting from the goal (a location and a date) and working back from there to work out when to leave: which airport is nearest our destination, which airport do

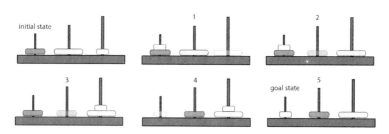

FIGURE 3.6 A mapping between a version of the ToH and the Monsters and Globes Change Problem (Hayes & Simon, 1977).

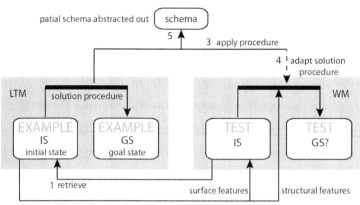

FIGURE 3.7 The processes involved in analogical problem-solving. While there is a number attached to each process, they should not be taken as being done entirely consecutively. E.g., mapping applying and adapting can be done iteratively.

we need to leave from, what time do we want to get there, how to get to the airport, what time do we have to leave. If it's a destination such as a holiday home you go to frequently then there is less planning to do and you can work forward. That is, you already know when to leave, how to get to the airport, what the flight times are, etc. The planning is a lot less effortful.

Have a look at the puzzle in Box 3.3.

The first idea most people have is to put, or imagine putting, six cannonballs on one side and six on the other and see what

---

BOX 3.3 THE CANNONBALLS PROBLEM

Imagine you have 12 cannonballs – a common occurrence. They all look alike but one is different in that it is either heavier or lighter than the others, but you don't know which. Imagine also that you are equipped a large balance scale that can hold any number of cannonballs on either side. Find the oddball using the scales a maximum of four times.

happens. Naturally, the scales will go down on one side since the oddball is there somewhere. As soon as that happens, most people then realize that weighing six cannonballs on either side tells them nothing since they don't know if there is a heavy ball weighing it down on one side or a light ball raising it up on the other. So, they are back to square one. What this shows is that a) there are WM limits to our ability to plan ahead, and b) failure can sometimes tell us something useful about a problem. Most people need to make that first erroneous move, at least mentally, before starting again with one that will lead them more directly to the solution. An even more important reason why problems are hard relates to the mental representations we form of a problem in the first place. Get that wrong and the problem may end up being insoluble. Changing representations to find a new effective way of solving a problem is the hallmark of creativity.

CREATIVE PROBLEM-SOLVING

There are some putative differences between 'normal' problem-solving and creative problem-solving. Many problems have a single solution in the sciences and the goal is to find it. These involve *convergent thinking* as the aim is to converge on the required solution – the correct answer, in other words. *Divergent thinking* can involve thinking of multiple possible solutions or exploring a number of options and is often taken as a proxy measure for creative thinking. The distinction was one made by Guilford (1950). There is also a false distinction made between the sciences and humanities where the sciences are seeking 'the answer' to a problem whereas in the arts, there are multiple answers in novels, paintings, films, and so on. However, this is to confuse an outcome with the process of getting there. There have been many immensely creative scientists, engineers, mathematicians, computer programmers, and so on.

Perhaps a better distinction between creative and everyday well-defined problem-solving is in terms of heuristics and algorithmic processes. Lubart and Mouchiraud (2003) referred to well-defined problems requiring learned procedures or algorithms as 'canned' problems. Creative problem-solving produces results or uses methods that are novel, valuable, and 'non-obvious' (Amabile, 1996; Simonton, 2011). So, how does one go about doing that? One way is to re-represent the problem, so instead of trying to solve a problem using previously learned methods – what Wertheimer (1945) referred to as *reproductive thinking* – an understanding of the underlying structure of the problem can lead to *productive thinking.* An example of this can be seen in Box 3.4.

Problems like the one in Figure 3.8 often require what is usually referred to as 'insight'. At first, one might try to represent the problem using previous knowledge (reproductive thinking) which would not be useful in this case. You reach an impasse. What's needed is a different way of representing the problem, perhaps by focussing on different features. If you are lucky, you might find a representation that leads directly to the goal, and you have an 'Aha!' experience. Gestalt psychologists like Wertheimer believed that insight was a special process as did some later psychologists (Metcalfe, 1986; Metcalfe & Wiebe, 1987). Others believed it could be explained in terms of everyday information processing (Kaplan & Simon, 1990; Ohlsson, 1992; Weisberg, 1986). For example, Ohlsson argued that, based on an initial representation of a problem such as the one in Figure 3.8, we search for mental operators that might apply. If that fails, we reach an impasse and the only way out is to seek another representation, and if that is a useful one then it triggers operators from LTM that we can apply, sometimes quite suddenly. Hence, the 'Aha!' experience.

BOX 3.4 THE ROSE WINDOW PROBLEM

The problem is to paint the light grey sections surrounding a cathedral's rose window in gold leaf. Unfortunately, gold leaf is very expensive so it's important to know exactly how much is required which, in turn, requires the painters to calculate the area of the light grey sections (see Figure 3.8).

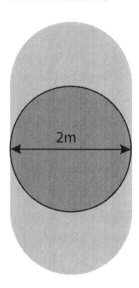

FIGURE 3.8 Calculate the area of the light grey walls. The solution is shown in Figure 3.9.

Another feature of Ohlsson's theory was constraint relaxation. Sometimes we impose constraints on problem-solving that are not there. In the film Men in Black, Will Smith finds himself with a group of applicants for what they believe is a branch of the FBI. They are made to sit in awkward soft armchairs, provided with sharp pencils and told to fill in a form. The Will Smith character realizes that the pencil just pierces and tears the paper so he drags over a very heavy table to his chair so that he can use it to lean on. He has identified an unconscious self-imposed constraint (just sit where you are and fill in the form) and removed it. Needless to say, he gets the job. Insight problems and creative problem-solving often involve getting over such self-imposed constraints. Constraints can also enhance creativity. My children's primary school tried to persuade pupils to walk to school and asked older pupils to write an essay describing their walk – what they saw, heard, or passed on their way. My children lived directly opposite the school gate, so they were obliged to be creative in what they wrote. Problem-solving

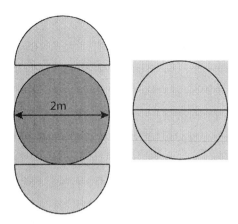

FIGURE 3.9 Solution to the Rose Window problem. The top and bottom of the window form two semicircles 2 meter in diameter. If you imagine them filling the dark circle, you end up with a square 2 meter by 2 meter. So, you need enough gold leaf to cover four square meters.

can therefore be aided by either removing constraints that were incorporated into the initial representation of a problem but weren't explicitly there, or by imposing constraints to enhance creativity such as those, say, in the haiku verse form.

SUMMARY

We are faced with problems of all kinds every day. Whenever you have a goal and you don't know immediately how to get there, you have a problem. A few are well-defined in that all the information needed to allow you to move through a problem space is provided. You know the initial state, what the goal state should look like, what you are allowed to do to work through the problem (mental operators), and what you are not allowed to do (restrictions or constraints). Most problems, however, are ill-defined and we have to work out what the operators might be and what restrictions there are, and the goal state might be very vaguely defined.

Problems can be hard because our cognitive system is 'bounded' – there are limits to WM, retrieving relevant information from LTM, and so on. They can be made a bit more manageable by breaking them down into sub-goals that are more tractable.

Analogical problem-solving means using a previous problem to help solve a current one. Solving many related problems in a particular domain such as architecture, radiography, and wine-making can lead to the development of a schema for the problem type and, eventually, expertise in the domain.

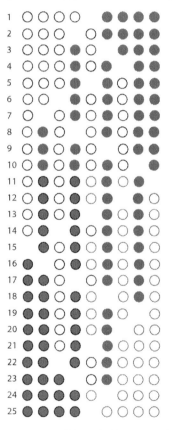

FIGURE 3.10 The solution procedure for the Eight Coins problem.

Creative problem-solving generally involves finding a novel or optimum way of representing a problem. Finding an appropriate analogy, as often happens in poetry, can produce a creative result. Removing constraints that aren't there or imposing new ones can both lead to novel outcomes. For a solution to be deemed creative, it has to be novel, of high quality, non-obvious, and valued by society.

SUGGESTED FURTHER READING

Newell, A., & Simon, H. A. (1972/2019). *Human problem solving* (reprint edition). Echo Point Books & Media.

Robertson, S. I. (2017). *Problem solving: Perspectives from cognition and neuroscience* (2nd ed.). Psychology Press.

Sternberg, R. J., Grigorenko, E. L., & Singer, J. L. (Eds.). (2004). *Creativity: From potential to realization.* American Psychological Association.

RATIONAL THINKING

INTRODUCTION

We like to think that we are rational animals capable of abstract thought. We rely on our ability to reach reasoned conclusions based on the facts before us. But just how rational are we? And, indeed, what does it mean to be rational? This chapter looks at what the rules of reasoned argument entail and the extent to which our everyday thinking conforms to them. The next chapter concentrates on the ways our thinking and reasoning are 'biased' and where we generally eschew Type 2 thinking, appropriately or otherwise, and rely on heuristics and intuition instead.

First, what does 'rational' mean? There are several ways the term 'rational' can be used:

- *Normative rationality*: we are rational insofar as we can derive a logical conclusion from the information we are given based on norms or rules. Past studies of human rationality have tended to examine the degree to which our conclusions are valid, consistent, and true. Evans (2002) has referred to this as the 'deduction paradigm'. Analyzing human thinking based on the formal theories of logical reasoning can indeed tell us something about human reasoning, mainly that it's not really what we do most of the time. Prior beliefs and desires have been seen to get in the way of this kind of rational thinking.

- *Instrumental rationality* is the degree to which our thinking allows us to achieve our goals and how we go about doing so. A version of this derives from an economic model of human choice according to which we make decisions that maximize our *expected utility*, which is a way of saying that we make decisions based on how much we expect a particular outcome will be useful, beneficial, or valuable to us either materially or psychologically.
- *Epistemic rationality* refers to our beliefs about the world, how we assess them, and update them based on new information. It includes our ability to refrain from believing propositions that are not based on evidence or that are unlikely based on the evidence you have.

We begin with a brief look at so-called normative views of rationality where human reasoning is contrasted with the rules of logic.

'LOGICAL' THINKING

What we think of as logical thinking can be demonstrated by our ability to derive a valid conclusion given a set of assertions, or general principles known as *premises*. In some familiar situations, we can do just that, but when faced with problems that are unfamiliar or abstract, we tend to find this type of reasoning more difficult. One reason for this is that the conclusion to a logical argument is due to its structure (its syntax) and is unaffected by the meaning (the semantics) of the premises. The most commonly used example of such an argument, known as a *syllogism*, is:

All men are mortal

Socrates is a man

Therefore, Socrates in mortal

The structure of the syllogism is:

All As are Bs

C is an A

Therefore, C is a B

You can, however, use this structure to reach a valid conclusion based on faulty premises. Take for example the set of statements:

All Frenchmen have two heads

Jean-Pierre is a Frenchman

Therefore Jean-Pierre has two heads

The conclusion is logically consistent and valid based on the initial premises but deemed false because its main premise, 'All Frenchmen have two heads', was false to begin with. There can, therefore, be a tension between a valid argument and what we know to be the case. You can generate all manner of logically correct conclusions based on faulty premises and you can find many examples in the assertions of politicians, journalists, and bloggers or in the actions of those that follow them:

Mexicans are rapists and drug dealers

My neighbour is a Mexican

Therefore, my neighbour is a rapist and drug dealer.

This would be a valid conclusion if one assumes the premises.

Box 4.1 has some other examples of problems that require logical reasoning to reach a valid conclusion:

BOX 4.1 LOGICAL PUZZLES

1. Harry is looking at Mary. Mary is looking at Jack. Harry is married. Jack is not. Is someone who is married looking at someone who is not? Is the answer 'yes', 'no' or 'you can't tell for sure'?
2. Which of the statements in the box is true?
    There is one, and only one, false statement in this box.
    There are two, and only two, false statements in this box.
    There are three, and only three, false statements in this box.
    There are four, and only four, false statements in this box.
3. Here are a couple of statements. What can you reasonably infer from them?

    All the men are athletes
    Some of the athletes are rich

    What, if anything, logically follows?

Problem 1 involves testing hypotheses such as 'if X is the case then what follows?'. We know Harry is married and Jack is not, but what about Mary? If Mary is married, and given that she is looking at Jack, then the answer in this case would be 'yes'. If Mary is not married, and given that Harry who is married is looking at her, then the answer here is also 'yes'.

In Problem 2, there is a reasonably quick answer or a more time-consuming one involving testing hypotheses. The latter strategy also goes along the lines of 'if X is the case then what follows?' until either the hypothesis is falsified or not. You could go through each statement and test it. 'There is one false statement in the box' can't be true because all four statements contradict each other. And so on. More simply, since there can only be one true statement, there must be three false statements, which is exactly what the third statement says.

In Problem 3, the first two statements are premises (let us assume for the moment that they are not themselves false). Now, many people will have concluded that 'some of the men are rich' is a logical conclusion based on these premises. We know that some men are athletes, and that some of them – some footballers, for example – are rich. It seems to make sense to conclude that some of the men must be rich.

The following set of premises is similar in structure to those in Problem 3 above.

All the men are athletes
Some of the athletes are women

What, if anything, logically follows?

Here 'rich' is replaced by 'women'. In this case, we would not reasonably conclude that some of the men must be women. The structure of the argument is identical to the previous one and follows the pattern:

All the As are Bs
Some of the Bs are Cs

(Invalid) conclusion: Some of the As are Cs

So, if you thought it was reasonable to infer that some of the men were rich, then you should equally infer that some of the men were women. The conclusion is not a valid one, no matter what the As, Bs, and Cs represent. It's a lot easier to simply use what we know about the world to come to a seemingly valid conclusion rather than looking for alternative interpretations. As a result, our world knowledge often overwhelms any concern for the structure of the argument.

As well as the misunderstandings caused by the word 'some' in arguments, 'not' can also confuse things somewhat. Here are some examples using 'not' in the second premise.

1.

All cats meow
Rover is not a cat

Conclusion: Rover does not meow
Is that a logical conclusion?

The conclusion looks correct because one might implicitly assume that cats and only cats meow. In the UK, Rover is a dog's name. We know cats meow and that dogs bark so concluding that Rover does not meow seems reasonable. Here's an example with an identical structure:

2.

All men are human beings
Beyoncé is not a man

Conclusion: Beyoncé is not a human being

Again, it's the structure of the argument in these cases that leads to a conclusion and not its content. The conclusion is not valid for Beyoncé and it's not valid for Rover either.

TYPES OF LOGICAL REASONING

Suppose you meet an alien entity called a Zugg. Let's also suppose, for the purposes of this illustration, that the Zugg 'squacks'. Later you come across another Zugg and discover that this Zugg also squacks. Later still yet another Zugg crosses your path and – lo and behold! – it too squacks. Sometime after that you meet a fourth Zugg called Gronad. What can you now reasonably assume about Gronad? Why, that it squacks, of course.

To reach that conclusion involves two kinds of reasoning. First, you must have generalized, from the specific examples of squacking Zuggs you have encountered, that Zuggs squack.

You don't even need to know what 'squack' means to reason this way. This kind of learning, through your experience of instances of a concept, is an example of *inductive reasoning* (see also Figure 3.7). However, you didn't stop there. A second type of reasoning enabled you to make the inference that Gronad could squack because you have learned from past examples that Zuggs squack. This kind of inference is a *deductive* one. Deductive inferences involve applying general rules or laws – what you have learned – to new instances of the learned concept. It is a rational way of reasoning: All Zuggs squack, Gronad is a Zugg, therefore Gronad squacks. It also allows you to assume the conjugation of the verb 'to squack'. When you encounter new verbs, you can apply what you know about the endings of verbs to the new instance.

Induction is a very powerful mechanism for learning from experience and we are very, very good at it. It is a way of estimating what a population is like based on the sample you have encountered. You end up with an implicit rule such as 'If it is a Zugg then it squacks'. From experience, we learn similarly that dogs bark, birds fly, swans are white, and so on. Unfortunately, inductive reasoning is not guaranteed to be correct. Some birds don't fly, some swans turn out to be black, and Zuggs don't exist. Furthermore, induction can be either conservative or liberal (or 'hasty'). If you encounter a Zugg and you recognize that it has certain properties including being greyish in colour, and you encounter a second one that has the features of the first but this one is almost black, is it still a Zugg? You might withhold judgement until you get more information. On the other hand, we can be pretty liberal with our inductions and generalize to what you think an entire population is like based on a single example (see also Chapter 6).

In the figures that follow, an arrow points to an implication (if it rains → I will get wet) or a state of affairs (→ it is raining). Figure 4.1 represents a situation where, if you encounter A (which could be a Zugg, or lying on a sunny beach, or a lump of coal) and find that it is always accompanied by B (the Zugg squacks; you get sunburn; the coal is black), then you induce a rule that says that when you have A, then you also have B

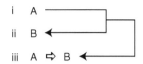

FIGURE 4.1 This represents the fact that when A is the case (line i) and B follows on from it (line ii) as a consequence, then you end up with iii which represents the rule that A implies B.

(if it's a Zugg, then it squacks; if you lie on a sunny beach, then you will get sunburn; if it's coal, then it's black). That is an inductive inference.

As a result of what you learn about the world through experience or through being told, you can develop rules of this kind. Some of them may well be in the form of a reasonable assumption (John is married to Ekaterina, therefore Ekaterina is married to John), a category (things that happen at committee meetings) or a learned stereotype (what you believe about fundamentalist Christians). Now, there are two things we can do: we can either obey the rule (accept the assumption or stereotype) or we can check whether the rule is indeed valid in which case you are treating the rule as a kind of hypothesis that you can test. Examples might be:

If it rains, then I will get wet
If I ruled the world, every man would be as free as a bird
If I eat my vegetables, then I will live longer

Let us assume for the moment that the statements (the premises) are true and that we want to check the logical consistency of any conclusion we derive from them. Based on such conditional (if...then) statements, we can work out whether something is the case or not. So:

1.
If it rains
Then I will get wet
Given: It is raining

What follows?
I will get wet.
2.
If I ruled the world
Then every man would be as free as a bird
Given: Every man is not as free as a bird
What follows?
I don't rule the world

Example 1 is valid. The rule says that if it rains then it must follow that I will get wet. Given that it is raining, it must follow that I will get wet. This form of reasoning is called *modus ponens*. It's not the kind of reasoning that we tend to get wrong.

Example 2 is valid. Every man is not as free as a bird; therefore, I don't rule the world because if I did rule the world, then every man would be as free as a bird. This is called *modus tollens.*

Here are some more examples. Again, assume for the sake of the exercise that the original premise in each case is correct. For each one, try to determine whether the conclusion given is valid or invalid.

3.
John keeps going out in the cold without a scarf. If he goes out without a scarf he will catch cold.
Given: John now has a cold
Conclusion: He has again gone out without a scarf. I did warn him!
4.
If you read this book your thinking will be improved
Given: Your thinking is not improved
Conclusion: You read the book, but it didn't help.
5.
If the animal in front of us meows, then it is a cat.
Given: It doesn't meow
Conclusion: It can't be a cat

Example 3 is invalid. John may have caught a cold due to not wearing a scarf or for reasons other than not wearing a scarf.

This is a logical fallacy known as *affirming the consequent* and is one that people fall into when it is disguised and sounds very plausible.

Example 4 is invalid. The statement says that if you read this book, then your thinking must be improved. Therefore, if it has not improved, then you can't have read the book. This is the same argument as Example 2 above. (Bear in mind that we are assuming the premises are correct…).

Example 5 is fallacious. It's the same argument as saying: 'If I fix people's plumbing then I am employed. I don't fix people's plumbing therefore I am unemployed'. There may be other reasons why the animal in Example 5 doesn't meow. This kind of argument is known as *denying the antecedent.*

We are capable of judging whether an argument is false or not, but it sometimes involves a lot of effort. It's a lot easier and less taxing on our poor old WM if we rely on what we are accustomed to, or what we know, or just what seems on the surface to be reasonable. The logical fallacy known as 'affirming the consequent' (Example 3) is one that we often fall for, but which can often be useful. If A implies B and B is the case, then there may be good reasons to suspect that A is probably the case as well, although this is not guaranteed. It is for this reason that Sherlock Holmes uses this 'logically invalid' method to reach his conclusions.

WHY SHERLOCK HOLMES' REASONING IS ILLOGICAL

The Sherlock Holmes character has often been assumed to be logical in his analysis of situations. Here are a couple of examples of his reasoning from two of Conan Doyle's stories.

> 'In solving a problem of this sort, the grand thing is to be able to reason backward. That is a very useful accomplishment, and a very easy one, but people do not practice it much. In the everyday affairs of life, it is more useful to reason forward, and so the other comes to be neglected. There are fifty who can reason synthetically for one who can reason analytically'.

'I confess', said I, 'that I do not quite follow you'.

'I hardly expected that you would. Let me see if I can make it clearer. Most people, if you describe a train of events to them, will tell you what the result would be. They can put those events together in their minds, and argue from them that something will come to pass. There are few people, however, who, if you told them a result, would be able to evolve from their own inner consciousness what the steps were which led up to that result. This power is what I mean when I talk of reasoning backward, or analytically'.

(Doyle, 1887, pp. 83–84, *A Study in Scarlet*)

So, what Sherlock Holmes means by people who reason 'synthetically' is that they can work out that B is the case whenever A is the case, i.e., modus ponens. Sherlock, however, argues here that he reasons 'analytically' and 'reasons backward' so that given B, then A should follow. As we have seen, this is *affirming the consequent*. It is a form of reasoning known as *abduction* (see Figure 4.2). An example of what can be derived using this form of logic is shown in the next example.

'I can see nothing', said I, handing [the hat] back to my friend.

'On the contrary, Watson, you can see everything. You fail, however, to reason from what you see. You are too timid in drawing your inferences'.

'Then, pray tell me what it is that you can infer from this hat?'

He picked it up and gazed at it in the peculiar introspective fashion which was characteristic of him. 'It is perhaps less suggestive than it might have been', he remarked, 'and yet there are a few inferences which are very distinct, and a few others which represent at least a strong balance of probability. That the man was highly intellectual is of course obvious upon the face of it, and also that he was fairly well-to-do within the last three years, although he has now fallen upon evil days. He had foresight, but has less now than formerly, pointing to a moral retrogression, which, when taken with the decline of his fortunes, seems to indicate some evil influence, probably drink, at work upon him. This may account also for the obvious fact that his wife has ceased to love him'.

'My dear Holmes!'

'He has, however, retained some degree of self-respect', he continued, disregarding my remonstrance. 'He is a man who leads a sedentary life, goes out little, is out of training entirely, is middle-aged, has grizzled hair which he has had cut within the last few days, and which he anoints with lime-cream. These are the more patent facts which are to be deduced from his hat. Also, by the way, that it is extremely improbable that he has gas laid on in his house'.

(Doyle, 1892, p. 246, *The Blue Carbuncle*)

So, where does Sherlock get these conclusions from? Here are a few of the features of the hat that he uses: The hat is expensive but now out of date and hasn't been replaced (so the owner has 'fallen upon evil days'). Sweat stains show he is out of training, several tallow drips from a candle suggest he does not have gas. The hat has not been brushed, therefore he does not now have a wife to either exhort him to brush it or to brush it for him. As with the case with 'if it rains then I will get wet. I am wet', there may well be other explanations for the details that Sherlock used to derive his conclusions. Maybe the man had stolen the hat, for instance. However, an abductive inference is an explanatory hypothesis and the likelihood of it being accurate depends on the quality of the explanation given (Lombrozo, 2012; Thagard, 1989). Important words in the last excerpt include 'probability', 'seems to indicate', 'probably', and 'improbable', which attests to the view that Conan Doyle was well aware that abductive reasoning can only be probabilistic. I am obviously using abductive reasoning here, though.

The three types of reasoning discussed are shown diagrammatically in Figure 4.2.

THE NEW PARADIGM

Early studies of human reasoning based on the rules of logic did not provide a true picture of the kinds of thinking that humans actually engage in. We rely on what we know about the world rather than, or along with, the syntactic structure

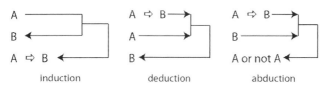

FIGURE 4.2 Diagrammatic representations of different forms of reasoning. In (a) if A is consistently followed by B, then assume A implies B (inductive inference). In (b) given that A implies B, and that A is the case, then B must also be the case (deductive inference). In (c) given that A implies B, and that B is the case, A may or may not be the case.

of arguments, a phenomenon known as *belief bias*. Since just before the beginning of the century, the focus of research in this area by psychologists has shifted away from the normative rules of logical inference to probabilistic judgements of what a reasonable inference might be, given a set of propositions or premises. This shift of focus has been referred to as a *new reasoning paradigm* (Elqayam & Evans, 2013) to contrast with the previous deduction paradigm (Evans, 2002). Rather than examining thinking in terms of validity, consistency or truth value, it examines it in terms of our uncertainties when thinking and making decisions. An outcome is not deemed to be binary (will happen – won't happen) but includes a degree of uncertainty (I'm really sure it will happen – I hope it might happen – it probably won't happen), and also what kind of value we place on the outcome (It is really desirable – it could be quite useful – it might be disastrous). It also emphasizes the relative values people place on actions and potential actions.

Elqayam & Evans (2013) describe the new paradigm as being a 'shift from truth to belief', from propositions that are either true or false to '*subjective probability*, in which the subject matter is human belief' and where reasoning and decision-making are subject to varying strengths of belief, uncertainty, and subjectivity (Elqayam & Evans, 2013; Elqayam & Over, 2013). People hold beliefs with varying degrees of confidence. Reasoning is, therefore, best understood by taking a Bayesian approach. When we learn to associate A with B through experience or the associations our culture presents us with, we can use them implicitly to make predictions. If our predictions are incorrect, this can lead to confusion. A man rushes to hospital with his son who has been injured. The boy is taken to the operating theatre and the surgeon comes out to look at him and says, 'I can't operate on him. He's my son'. If most of the surgeons you have encountered or seen on TV or read about in books are male, then that is the assumption you might make based on prior probabilities. This story is less confusing than it was 40 years ago when there were fewer female surgeons. Bayes' rule is a way of establishing how our prior beliefs or expectations can change as new information comes to light.

Although Bayes' theorem can be used to model changes in beliefs over time with new information, we human beings do not always incorporate new information into our thinking. We diverge from a strict Bayesian description of beliefs and decisions and hence are irrational in that respect. We exhibit biases in our thinking based on prior beliefs that are held quite strongly and when new information is presented that contradict those beliefs we are liable to ignore it or find ways to discredit it. For a person who believes strongly in a God, the prior probability (p) of such a belief would be $p = 1$. Someone else might have no belief in gods, and so the prior probability of such a belief is $p = 0$. Donald Trump is someone who does not believe that climate change is real. Volume II of the Fourth National Climate Assessment reported that climate change in the US was already affecting or would affect the environment, the economy, energy production, ecosystems, human health and welfare, and land and water resources. The report was compiled by thousands of people referencing thousands more researchers. Donald Trump said, 'I don't believe it'. His beliefs were not updated after new information was obtained. Sticking to a belief despite contradictory evidence or actively trying to discredit the evidence is an example of confirmation bias and is discussed more fully in the next chapter.

'RATIONAL' DECISIONS AND WHEN TO AVOID THEM

Being fully instrumentally rational means choosing an option that maximizes out *subjective utility*. However, there are limits on our ability to do so, such as our limited WM capacity, so we constrain the information we process. There are also uncertainties involved in analyzing one option over another. The kind of reasoning this entails is generally an attempt to weigh up the pros and cons of a decision, bearing in mind that there may well be unconscious as well as conscious influences on what constitutes the various pros and cons. As a result, we rely on heuristics and biases in the ways we think. However, if one were to make the conscious effort to be as rational as possible in our decision-making, what would that involve? Suppose you have to make a decision about something important such as asking someone to marry you or buying a car. Given their relative importance, it would be reassuring to think that such decisions, although subjective, are based on some analysis of the pros and cons or the costs and benefits to us of a particular outcome. A rational model of decision-making assumes we can rank various preferences. For example, in buying a house, we might rank the room sizes as being probably more important than the garden size, or the kitchen layout as more important than the size of the main bedroom, or whatever. Another assumption is that we try to look at all the available information and use it to work out the probability of success – in this case, choosing the best house from the ones on offer – given that there is a degree of uncertainty about much of the information we use.

One view of human rationality from economics, the *Homo Economicus* model, was based on the idea that people try to maximize their expected utility. According to this, people use all the information they have access to. Furthermore, we have consistent preferences and we tend to avoid biases in processing the information available (for more details see Corr & Plagnol, 2019). There is even an equation that can be used to calculate the expected utility of an outcome:

$$EU[A] = \Sigma_{i=1}, \ldots, np(x_i|A)U(x_i)$$

where U is the utility of a particular state and EU is the Expected Utility of an action or decision (A) where the outcome is uncertain. X is the state reached after performing the action A and has a number of values (x_1 to x_n) and a distribution (p_1 to p_n).

So, every time you decide to buy a sofa, you sit down with a scientific calculator and work out the expected utility of buying this sofa. Don't you? Well, perhaps not. You could, however, do something simpler such as list the pros and cons of buying the sofa and giving each one a weight, positive and negative. Add them up and *voilà*. Although it appears reasonable, in real life, things don't quite work like that. Have a look at the scenario in Box 4.2 where this mechanism is applied. It contains an example of what Corr and Plagnol (p. 89) referred to as 'more Homer (Simpson) than homo economicus'.

So, a rational approach to decision-making in situations like this is probably not going to work. Indeed, in the early stages of a romantic relationship, we can be very attuned to the benefits but very blind to the costs. Juliet didn't seem to pay all that much attention to the cons of running off with Romeo, nor did Paris perform a cost-benefit analysis of abducting Helen and carting her off to Troy. This isn't to say that we don't make good choices, but rather that we don't use all available information and we don't compute a rational choice from that information because we don't have time to do all that thinking. And most of the time, we don't need to. What we do instead is make a quick decision based on limited criteria and choose the first one that meets those criteria. This is called *satisficing* (Simon, 1956). It means choosing an outcome (a restaurant, or a car, or a partner) that is good enough. Although the word is often attributed to him, it is a Northumbrian word reflecting the fact that our decisions are often made based on the degree to which they satisfy some criteria and on the extent to which they, in turn, suffice in allowing us to achieve a goal. Another example would be when you're on holiday in an unfamiliar town. It's the evening, you're hungry, and you want something to eat. You wander along the town centre looking

BOX 4.2 HOW NOT TO SWEET TALK YOUR PARTNER

"Hi, Jennifer?"

"Yes?"

"Hi, it's George."

"Oh, hello love, I didn't recognize your voice for a moment. How are you?"

"Great. Listen, I had a really great time the other night."

"Mmmm. me too."

"So, what I've done is ... I've been trying to work out how profitable this relationship is likely to be."

"Huh?"

"What I've done is I've drawn up a list of all the rewards I can get out of our relationship and put a rough figure beside each one and then I've done the same with the costs. But listen, the great thing is when I subtract the costs from the rewards I'm still left with quite a high figure. Isn't that great?"

"Are you having me on George?"

"No really. I'll read out some of my list. You should do one of your own, too, to see what you think. Ok, so. Rewards first. No particular order here: You look good, 10 points; you've got really good taste, 6 points; you seem to like the same activities as me, 6 points; you're good in bed, 15 points; you do that thing I like, you know the one ... anyway that has to be worth a good 12 points. You've ..."

"George ..."

"No wait, there's more. On the costs side, right? I've got: My mum doesn't like you, 7 points; you don't earn much money, 8 points; you spend a fortune on clothes – that'll have to be 10 points, I'm afraid."

"George!"

"Yeah?"

[Click. Dialling tone]

"Jennifer? Jennifer?"

at the numerous restaurants available. It would take a very long time to examine and compare all the menus and the ambiance and so on. You might compare just a few and settle on one that meets some criteria of your choosing (price, dishes on offer, background music not too loud, etc.). Satisficing can be regarded as a rational strategy in a world where we don't have access to all the information or time to process it all. We can make the best use of what we've got instead. Our rationality is limited and spending time and effort working things out 'rationally' is often unnecessary and sometimes counterproductive. Most of the time, it is enough to rely on heuristics and habits. Some heuristics allow us to make fast and reasonably accurate judgements. Others can take the form of 'biases' in thinking where our thinking is suboptimal. This is the subject of the next chapter.

SUMMARY

There are different ways of defining rationality, the main ones being normative rationality where human reasoning can be judged by the criteria of logical norms, and instrumental rationality judged by the extent to which our thinking allows us to achieve our goals. Both are linked to our beliefs about the world (epistemic rationality).

Syllogisms involve a number of assertions (premises) leading to a conclusion based on the structure of the argument – its syntax – rather than its content – its semantics. The simplest structure that we tend to get correct is modus ponens – if A is the case and A implies B, then B must follow otherwise A would not imply B. Similarly, if B is not the case and A implies B, then A can't be the case either (modus tollens). We are less accurate at detecting the invalidity in such cases.

Induction is the process by which we learn about the world. Once a rule or category is learned, it can be applied to new instances through deductive inference. Abductive reasoning is based on the likelihood of A given B even if A is not a strictly valid conclusion.

The New Paradigm takes human beliefs and updating evidence into account based on Bayesian probabilities and the extent to which people take prior and posterior probabilities into account in their thinking. If people do not update their beliefs based on new evidence, no matter how overwhelming that evidence is, then they may end up deriving false conclusions, and making errors of judgement.

A rational model of human decision-making was proposed by classical economists based on the assumption that people tried to maximize their expected utility. However, humans are not always very good at doing so. There was, therefore, a shift to behavioural economics and the heuristics and biases approach to thinking.

SUGGESTED FURTHER READING

Elqayam, S., & Evans, J. S. B. T. (2013). Rationality in the new paradigm: Strict versus soft Bayesian approaches [Article]. *Thinking & Reasoning*, *19*(3/4), 453–470. https://doi.org/10.1080/13546783.2013.834268

Evans, J. S. B. T. (2017). *Thinking and reasoning: A very short introduction*. Oxford, UK: Oxford University Press.

Manktelow, K. (2012). *Thinking and reasoning*. London, UK: Routledge.

Stanovich, K. E., West, R. F., & Toplak, M. E. (2013). Myside bias, rational thinking, and intelligence. *Current Directions in Psychological Science*, *22*(4), 259–264. https://doi.org/10.1177/0963721413480174

PART 3
WHEN THINKING GOES AWRY

BIASES, ERRORS, AND HEURISTICS

CONFIRMATION BIAS

If you have a belief or assumption about people, objects, situations or whatever, you are likely to notice events or instances that back up that belief or assumption. For example, people mainly read the kinds of blogs, newspapers, Facebook pages, and tweets that say the kinds of things they agree with. You make friends with people who have the same general attitudes as you. When newspapers hear about some finding or other and want to report it, they will often look for examples to back it up. They are unlikely to look for examples that contradict the thrust of their story. Some time ago, there was a newspaper report based on a research finding that successful women in high-power jobs tended to have male offspring. The papers then showed some photographs of successful women in powerful positions who had given birth to boys. They did not provide names or photographs of women in high-profile jobs who had girls.

The tendency to focus on information that appears to back up our beliefs, attitudes, and prejudices is known as *confirmation bias*, since we do not normally seek to disconfirm them. That said there are some contexts where a belief or hypothesis can be either confirmed or disconfirmed. For example, in law courts, prosecutors present evidence to show that a person is guilty of a crime and defenders present evidence to show that the person is innocent. Scientific method relies on testing a hypothesis on the assumption that there might be evidence against it. If you fail to disconfirm the hypothesis, then you have evidence for it (although not proof). In both cases, law and science, it is the system that ensures that bias is, at least, reduced.

EARLY STUDIES OF CONFIRMATION BIAS

The study of confirmation bias in psychology had its biggest impact in the 1960s when Peter Wason argued that people generally sought to confirm their hypotheses rather than to refute them. A classic study by Wason (1960) was the decision task which involved checking whether a rule was being obeyed. There are many variants, some concrete and some abstract. (The original concrete one used a rule about postage rates in Britain at the time where letters that were sealed required a different postage stamp from letters that were unsealed. Strange but true.) The 'abstract' version goes along the lines of the following: There are four cards with letters on one side and numbers on the other. There is a rule that says that if there is a vowel on one side, then there should be an even number on the other. Which card or cards should you turn over to find out if the rule is being obeyed? The situation is shown in Figure 5.1.

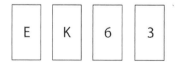

FIGURE 5.1 The Wason decision task.

Most people (about 45% according so some studies) pick the E and the 6 cards. Around 35% pick just the E card. A small number (around 7%) choose the E, 6, and 3 cards. About 4% choose the E and 3 cards. The rest pick a different combination. Let's take them one at a time: The E is a vowel so if there is an even number on the other side, then the rule is being obeyed; if there is an odd number, then it is being disobeyed. So, checking the E card is a good idea. The K card could have either an odd or an even number since the rule does not mention consonants. Turning the 6 card over could yield a vowel or a consonant but the rule refers only to what happens when there is a vowel – so the 6 card doesn't tell you anything about whether the rule is being obeyed or disobeyed. If you turn over the 3 card and find a vowel then you have shown that the rule is being disobeyed. So, the ones you should turn over are the E and the 3 cards.

As we saw, only about 4% of people get the answer right in this abstract version, but if it is reworded as a more concrete or familiar situation, the choice becomes obvious. Since a version involving postage stamps is no longer familiar, a different everyday version of the task is shown in Figure 5.2. You are a policeman and you are in a pub checking for underage drinking. If a person is under 18, then they should not be drinking an alcoholic drink. There is a table at which are seated a 15 year old and a 45 year old with drinks in front of them, and on the table close by are another two people with another two drinks – a coke and a whisky. What do you check to find out if the rule is being obeyed? In this case, most people have no problem. You would check who is drinking the whisky and what the fifteen year old is drinking to make sure it's not alcoholic. You are not interested in the 45-year nor in who is

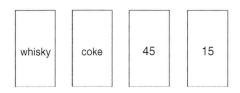

FIGURE 5.2 A concrete version of the Wason task.

drinking the Coke. However, both the abstract version and the concrete one are identical in their structure, so in the abstract version you should turn over the E and the 3 which maps on to the whisky and the 15 year old to see if the rule is being obeyed.

There is a lot more going on psychologically speaking in this task than meets the eye, and many explanations have been put forward for the difficulty of one version versus the easiness of the other. Some have argued that, despite finding the abstract version difficult, we are capable of logical reasoning since we can manage the concrete one. Yet, that simply suggests that we have mechanisms for dealing with specific contexts in the social environment such as permissions and prohibitions (Cheng & Holyoak, 1985) that we have either evolved to deal with or have learned to deal with through repeated experience. If we could deal with the abstract case and hence apply it to any version of the same problem structure, that would make us rational in the logical sense. But we don't. So, we're not. Arguably.

GUESSING WHEN TO STOP DIGGING

There is plenty of other evidence that we tend to use strategies that confirm our beliefs or assumptions rather than finding ways to refute them. So why have we evolved this apparently irrational way of thinking? The simple reason is that it is a very useful heuristic. You have an idea about something, you find what seems to be evidence supporting your idea, so that's fine. Once you have found information supporting your belief then you can stop digging. It's a very quick way of checking things. Searching for counter examples is effortful and time-consuming. Once you have seen several swans, you can reasonably conclude that swans are white. How much effort are you going to put in to check you haven't made a mistake (see Taleb, 2008)?

While heuristics are very useful methods for finding things out, they are not *guaranteed* to get the correct result. Just because every swan you have ever seen anywhere you have looked is white, that doesn't mean there aren't swans of a different colour where you haven't looked. When we look at some real-life examples, we see that things can really go awry. For example, confirmation bias can lead to a form of *selective attention* or *selective observation.* At a noisy party, we can selectively focus our attention on what someone is saying to us and ignore all the other conversations around us. Similarly, we are very good at paying attention to those events or objects that support our views and ignore those that do not. If you think that female drivers are poorer than male drivers, then you will notice it when a woman bangs into something, or performs a dangerous manoeuvre, or fails to reverse into a parking space, or whatever. You will *not* notice the sex of the driver when a man does it because that's not relevant to your prejudice. A prejudice is a pre-conceived belief that is not necessarily backed up by evidence or even your own experience because some aspects of that experience get filtered out. The 'base rate' of poor-driving-incidents-that-you-generally-notice over a certain period is ignored. Your prejudice, should you have such a one, primes you to notice the incident when a woman is at fault, and, what is more, the incident is evidence for your belief. QED.

You will also find it in a CV or job application when you choose what to put in and what to omit. Politics thrives on it and you can encounter it in the newspapers every day. One group of politicians, economists, and journalists might look at economic data and pick out the bits that show that the economy is doing well and another group will look at the same data and pick out the bits that show that the economy is failing. We also expect a degree of consistency in the world. Finding out that some small part of our belief system is out of kilter with the rest of it is uncomfortable and dealing with it may require a re-examination of the entire belief system. And that's not something most of us find easy to do (see Chapter 8).

DEALING WITH UNCERTAINTY

We rely on heuristics because we do not live in a world where all outcomes are certain or where all the information we need is available. Animals also use heuristics when making decisions. Gigerenzer and Brighton (2009), for example, give the example of a peahen which does not weigh up the pros and cons of every available peacock to determine the one with the 'highest expected utility'. Rather she picks the one with the largest number of eye spots on its tail feathers. This has proved to be an extremely effective and efficient evolutionary strategy. The more eyespots the peacock has, the fitter it is likely to be. The idea that we don't have to analyze all the available evidence to make a decision was exemplified by Simon (1956) where he pointed out that most everyday decisions involve this kind of satisficing.

While there have been very many studies into heuristics and biases, two groups stand out that take different views on heuristics and rationality. In the early 1970s, Daniel Kahneman and Amos Tversky (e.g., 1974) presented a range of ways in which our thinking is not always optimal heralding a new field of study into heuristics and biases in human thinking. In the 1990s, Gigerenzer, Todd, and the ABC Research Group (1999) emphasized the important and effective role that heuristics play in decision-making. In a footnote in the book 'Risk Savvy', Gigerenzer writes: 'It is sometimes said that for Kahneman, the glass of rationality is half-empty, and for Gigerenzer, the glass is half-full. One is a pessimist, the other an optimist. That characterization misses the point. We differ in what the glass of rationality is in the first place' (Gigerenzer, 2014, p. 282). Each group has its own 'favourite' heuristics which are deemed to be fairly universal. For Tversky and Kahneman, these are the *representativeness* and *availability* heuristics, and *anchoring and adjustment*. Gigerenzer and Todd, meanwhile, emphasize heuristics based on the idea that *less-is-more*. These are heuristics that can be very effective when information is lacking.

TVERSKY AND KAHNEMAN – BIASES AND HEURISTICS

REPRESENTATIVENESS

One of the ways in which we categorize objects and people is through what Tversky and Kahneman refer to as representativeness: 'when A is highly representative of B, the probability that A originates from B is judged to be high. On the contrary, if A is not similar to B, the probability that A originates from B is judged to be low' (Tversky & Kahneman, 1974, p. 1124). Kahneman and Tversky (1973) conducted a number of experiments on the representativeness heuristic. In one, the participants in one group (the low engineer group) are told that personality tests have been administered to 30 engineers and 70 lawyers and that thumbnail descriptions have been written for them. Participants are then given one of them:

Jack is a 45-year-old man. He is married and has four children. He is generally conservative, careful, and ambitious. He shows no interest in political and social issues and spends most of his free time on his many hobbies which include home carpentry, sailing, and mathematical puzzles.

The probability that Jack is one of the 30 engineers in the sample of 100 is ___ %. (p. 241)

The description does not contain any explicit reference to his occupation, but it does contain stereotypical features of an engineer. Participants in another group (the high engineer group) are told that there are 70 engineers and 30 lawyers. For the first group, the odds that Jack is an engineer is 3/7 and for the second it is 7/3. However, in both cases, participants ignored these prior probabilities and both groups made essentially the same probability judgements. Participants who were given no description predicted that Jack was an engineer only 30% of the time in the low engineer group, and those in the high engineer group predicted that he was an engineer 70% of the time. Strangely, perhaps, even an uninformative description led the participants to ignore the base rates: 'Dick is a 30-year-old man. He is married with no children. A man of high ability and high motivation, he promises to be quite successful in his field. He is well liked by his colleagues' (Kahneman & Tversky, 1973, p. 242). The likelihood that this person was an engineer was estimated by both groups to be 50/50.

In 1982, Tversky and Kahneman presented another famous study in psychology which has not only made its way into textbooks but also into works of fiction. In this study, people were given a statement describing someone and then asked to rank a list of items in terms of their probability based on that description. One of the statements read:

> Linda is 31 year old, single, outspoken, and very bright. She majored in philosophy. As a student, she was deeply concerned with issues of discrimination and social justice, and also participated in antinuclear demonstrations. Please check off the most likely alternative:

The items people had to rank included, amongst others: *Linda is a teacher in elementary school; Linda is active in the feminist movement; Linda is a bank teller.* In some versions, Tversky and Kahneman reduced the choices to just these two:

> 'Linda is a bank teller'.

> 'Linda is a bank teller and is active in the feminist movement'.

The participants in various versions of the study were likely to rank 'Linda is a bank teller and is active in the feminist movement' above 'Linda is a bank teller'. This ranking is irrational. The set of people who are bank tellers must be greater than the set of people who are bank tellers and active in the feminist movement as in Figure 5.3.

They referred to this as the *conjunction fallacy* where combining the two features is seen by participants as more likely than a single feature. To point out the fallacy, Manktelow (2012) likened this to saying that there are 'more guard dogs than dogs'.

In a review of a number of studies in 1982, Tversky and Kahneman (1982, p. 298) stated that 'Subjects ranked the outcomes based on the degree to which they matched the stereotypes'. Although this is referred to as the conjunction fallacy in the case of the Linda scenario, or failing to pay attention to the base rate in the case of Jack, when people are reading these descriptions, they are trying to get as much information out of

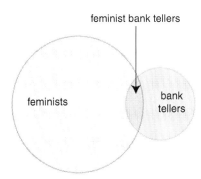

FIGURE 5.3 A representation of the space of feminists and the space of bank tellers and the conjunction between them.

them as possible by applying their knowledge of the world in the form of schemas or stereotypes triggered by the descriptions. So, if Linda happens to be a bank teller, the description of her as being concerned with issues of discrimination and social justice suggests that it is not unreasonable for her to be active in the feminist movement as well. So here, what Tversky and Kahneman refer to as intuition trumps logic.

As we have seen, the representativeness heuristic can cause people to ignore the base rate (e.g., the proportion of engineers to lawyers). Hence, Tversky and Kahneman (1971) suggested that many people had mistaken intuitions about the laws of chance. They tend to assume, for example, that a sample should have the same properties as the population from which it has come, based on the representativeness heuristic. They referred to this as the belief in the *law of small numbers*. A simple example of this uses coin tosses where the proportion of heads to tails in a short sequence of coin tosses may not match the proportion you would get in a long sequence of tosses. This is the *law of large numbers*. You cannot expect a short run of heads and tails to represent a long run. Figure 5.4 shows a number of coin tosses. The first selection shows three heads and three tails in a 'random' order. The other two sets of coin tosses do not represent the randomness of the long sequence and so

HTTHTHHHTTTHTTTHHHHTHTHTHTHTTTTTTTTHHTTTHHTHTHTHTHTTT

FIGURE 5.4 A number of coin tosses from a long run which three short run samples have been highlighted.

people might be tempted to think that they are not in fact randomly generated. People who make inferences on this basis are using the representativeness heuristic.

Tversky and Kahneman (1974) provide another example where their subjects ignored the sample size despite it being emphasized. In the description below, there is a small hospital and a larger one with the average number of births being greater for the larger one than the smaller one:

> A certain town is served by two hospitals. In the larger hospital about 45 babies are born each day, and in the smaller hospital about 15 babies are born each day. As you know, about 50% of all babies are boys. However, the exact percentage varies from day to day. Sometimes it may be higher than 50%, sometimes lower.
>
> For a period of one year, each hospital recorded the days on which more than 60% of the babies born were boys. Which hospital do you think recorded more such days?
>
> • The larger hospital (21);
> • The smaller hospital (21);
> • About the same (that is, within 5% of each other) (53).

The values in parentheses are the number of undergraduate students who chose each answer. Here again, a small sample is likely to veer away from the average seen in a large sample. The larger the sample, the closer it gets to the full population which, like the coin tosses, is going to be approximately 50% boys and 50% girls. However, most of the students picked the third option. Tversky and Kahneman (1974, p. 1125) concluded: 'This fundamental notion of statistics is evidently not part of people's repertoire of intuitions'.

Another related heuristic that Tversky and Kahneman (1974, p. 1127) have analyzed is the availability heuristic. This is a rule of thumb where we 'assess the frequency of a class or the probability of an event by the ease with which instances or occurrences can be brought to mind'. A simple example of this is from a paper in 1973: 'Are there more words in the English language that have the letter R as the first letter or as the third letter?' People find it easier to call to mind words beginning with R than with R as the third letter and so the ease with which they recall words biases their judgement.

It seems common sense to base our judgements on the information that comes most readily to mind and hence stands out. That information is, therefore, salient and available to use in making decisions or judgements. Unfortunately, in this complicated old world of ours, we may not have access to all the relevant information about a topic. You might read about a celebrity involved in some scandal in a newspaper but fail to read the subsequent apology in a small paragraph inside the paper a few days later essentially saying the story was untrue. As a result, what you think you know about the celebrity will be wrong (see Chapter 8). At the turn of the century, there were 'greatest' lists such as the greatest films of the 20th century. These tended to be ones from the second half of the century as they were relatively recent and hence the ones most readily recalled. To give another example, if what comes to mind are the images on TV of a child with autism who had an measles, mumps and rulella (MMR) vaccine shortly before and whose parents believe there is a causal link between the two, that may be the information that comes to mind when the MMR vaccine is later discussed.

Another example is given by Gigerenzer (2014). After the 9/11 terrorist attacks on the Twin Towers in New York and the Pentagon, people became reluctant to fly to distant destinations and chose instead to drive. When people tried to assess how safe it was to fly, the plane crashes were what readily came to mind and influenced their decisions. He estimated that approximately

1600 extra people lost their lives in road traffic accidents due to their decision to avoid flying.

ANCHORING AND ADJUSTMENT

Another important heuristic identified by Tversky and Kahneman (1974) was the anchoring and adjustment heuristic. It refers to a phenomenon whereby, when people are asked to judge a number such as a date, a time, or a distance, and a number is presented beforehand, they tend to provide an estimate that is influenced by this previously presented number. Tversky and Kahneman gave a number of simple examples of the heuristic at work. One involved asking participants to estimate the percentage of African countries in the UN. The experiment used a rigged wheel of fortune that generated a number such as 10 or 65 and the participants were asked to say whether the percentage was higher or lower than that number. Those who were asked to compare it to 10 produced an estimate of 25% whereas those who were given 65 as an anchor gave 45% as an estimate. In another example, one group was asked to guess quickly the product of the numbers 1 to 8, i.e., $1 \times 2 \times 3 \times 4 \times 5 \times 6 \times 7 \times 8$. Another was asked to guess the product of $8 \times 7 \times 6 \times 5 \times 4 \times 3 \times 2 \times 1$. They are, of course the same, but the low numbers at the start of the first sequence produced a median estimate of 512 whereas those who saw the sequence beginning with 8 produces 2,250 as a median estimate. (The correct answer is 40,320.) In these instances, participants were making an insufficient adjustment to generate their answers.

There have been many replications of the anchoring and adjustment effect and it is used by salespeople trying to sell double glazing, to give one example. 'The normal price for your windows is \$5200 (the anchor) but we can offer a reduction to \$4700. And if you choose to buy today, I can get you a price of \$4200 although I'd have to clear that with the manager'. The final price is quite a drop from the original anchor and hence seems like a relative bargain.

What has been unclear from the original studies of the heuristic is how the adjustment is computed by the participant. Epley and

Gilovich (2006) conducted experiments to identify the origins of the adjustment and why they were insufficient. They found evidence that people stop adjusting when they reach an 'implicit range of plausible values', a form of satisficing. They also found evidence that adjustment is effortful and hence people stop thinking further when a plausible estimate is reached. If people are encouraged to seek more appropriate estimates, then this weakens the magnitude of the anchoring bias.

GIGERENZER, TODD AND THE ABC RESEARCH GROUP – FAST AND FRUGAL HEURISTICS

Gigerenzer, Todd and the ABC Research Group (1999) have argued that the idea that there are systematic irrational fallacies in human reasoning due to the violation of normative rules of logic or probability is not the most useful way of understanding human thinking and decision-making. They argue that heuristics are used to make reasonable adaptive inferences about the world due to the constraints of time and lack of knowledge. In a view similar to that of Cosmides and Tooby (2011; Tooby & Cosmides, 2015, see Chapter 2), they argue that we have an adaptive toolbox containing specific cognitive mechanisms designed for different domains of inference. 'Fast and frugal heuristics that are matched to particular environmental structures allow organisms to be ecologically rational. The study of ecological rationality thus involves analyzing the structure of environments, the structure of heuristics, and the match between them' (Gigerenzer & Todd, 1999, p. 18). Instead of Homo Economicus, we therefore have *Homo Heuristicus*.

The simplest heuristic they introduce is the *recognition heuristic* which relies on a lack of knowledge for it to be useful: 'If one of two objects is recognized and the other is not, then infer that the recognized object has the higher value' (p. 41). In one study, they asked students at the University of Chicago and University of Munich to decide which of two cities was the largest in both the United States and Germany. San Diego was chosen by 62% of the

University of Chicago students as being larger than San Antonio; however, 100% of the German students chose correctly since they were unfamiliar with San Antonio. The American students were not ignorant enough to be able to use the recognition heuristic. (The proportions have since changed San Antonio now had 1.53 million inhabitants and San Diego had 1.43 million in 2020.)

Gigerenzer et al. applied this heuristic to a wider set of choices: stocks in the German and US stock markets. They asked experts in the US and in Germany and pedestrians in the streets in both countries which companies they recognized from a list on the US and German stock exchanges. A larger number were recognized by the experts than by the laypeople in both countries as one would expect. The most recognized companies by lay people were used as the basis for a test of the recognition heuristic. In a perhaps remarkable demonstration of trust in their theory, Gigerenzer and a colleague invested a substantial sum of money based on those companies chosen by people asked at random shopping in a German market. Over a six-month period, they tested the performance of the recognition heuristic against: a subset of companies that had not been recognized, the market index, mutual funds managed by professional portfolio managers, and a chance portfolio of randomly chosen companies. Overall, the recognition heuristic outperformed all other measures of stock market performance. When asked to pick companies in which non-experts might choose to invest their money, ignorance of the strength or otherwise of companies leads them to use a proxy measure for what to invest in, in this case how well they are recognized, mainly through the ubiquity of their products or ads. Kahneman and Frederick (2002) have referred to this as *attribute substitution* where, when one is faced with some aspect of a choice to be made ('which companies will enhance my investment?' – the target attribute), a simpler related property is chosen instead ('which companies have I heard of?' – the heuristic attribute).

Gigerenzer (2014) provides a dramatic example of where a single heuristic can be much more successful than examining detailed information. The episode is shown in the film 'Sully'. In January 2009, US Airways flight 1549 had taken off from LaGuardia airport in New York, then a flight of geese damaged both engines, with the result that the plane was now gliding. They turned back to try to make it to the airport but instead of trying to perform complex calculations about speed, distance, wind speed, etc., they used a simple gaze heuristic where they kept their gaze on the airport tower. If the tower appears to rise in the windshield, which it did, then they were not going to make it. As a result of relying on this one piece of information, they ditched their plane in the Hudson river instead and everyone survived. 'Will we make it back to the airport?' becomes 'Will the conning tower rise in the windshield?'

SUMMARY

Confirmation bias is ubiquitous but can be a useful heuristic to check whether an opinion, belief, rule or hunch is likely to be correct. An attempt at disconfirmation would be more effective but may be too difficult or time consuming. Heuristics are necessary as not all relevant information is available and we are often faced with a degree of uncertainty. Tversky and Kahneman discuss a number of heuristics and biases in particular:

- the representativeness heuristic – a simple computation based on the probability that an object or event A originates from class B by looking at the degree to which A is similar to B;
- the availability heuristic – where we assess the frequency or likelihood of an event based on the ease with which instances come to mind;
- Anchoring and adjustment – numerical judgements or estimates are often found to be based on a number that has just been presented.

Gigerenzer and Todd and the ABC Research Group argue that we have an 'adaptive toolbox' containing specific cognitive mechanisms covering different domains of inference, involving 'fast and frugal heuristics'. Some heuristics are based on the idea that 'less is more'. An example is the recognition heuristic – 'If one of two objects is recognized and the other is not, then infer that the recognized object has the higher value'.

SUGGESTED FURTHER READING

Gigerenzer, G., Hertwig, R., & Pachur, T. (Eds.). (2011). *Heuristics: The foundations of adaptive behavior*. Oxford, UK: Oxford University Press.
Kahneman, D. (2011). *Thinking, fast and slow*. London, UK: Penguin.
Taleb, N.N. (2008). *The black swan*. London, UK: Penguin.

6

SOCIETY MADE ME DO IT

INTRODUCTION

The representativeness heuristic comes into play when we rely on stereotypes to make judgements such as the probability that a particular person from a defined group has a particular attribute. A stereotype is a collection of associated attributes learned from experience and through cultural transmission. 'Having a stereotype doesn't make you a racist, sexist, or whatever-ist. It just means your brain is working properly, noticing patterns, and making generalizations' (Payne, Niemi, & Doris, 2018). It is, therefore, very useful but sometimes misleading. Thus, if all the plumbers you have encountered are male, then maleness would be a default attribute when you think of a plumber. Much of the time, this would be a useful culturally derived heuristic which is also indistinguishable from a bias (Hinton, 2017a, 2017b). Representativeness can work in two directions. An individual from a particular group is deemed to inherit the attributes of the group stereotype and hence represent it (see [a] in Figure 6.1). Alternatively, the attributes of a person from a group one is not particularly familiar with can be assumed to represent the attributes of the group (see [b] in Figure 6.1).

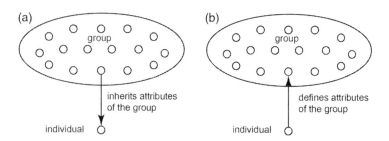

FIGURE 6.1 In (a), an individual from a particular circumscribed group is deemed to inherit the presumed attributes of the group (a stereotype). In (b), the attributes of an individual are deemed to be representative of an unfamiliar group the individual comes from.

For example, if you meet a grumpy Bulgarian with no sense of humour, you might conclude: 'Gosh, aren't Bulgarians grumpy and humourless'. This is an example of the 'liberal induction' we encountered in Chapter 4. Similarly, if a member of a group does something blameworthy, then the group in general may be seen as collectively to blame as often happens, for example, to Muslims. Chinese students in the UK and mainland Europe received racist comments or were even attacked because of the coronavirus pandemic. They somehow 'inherited the attribute' of having the virus due to being part of the same ethnic group as those Chinese citizens 5,000 miles away who had the virus. In April 2020, ISIS gunmen and suicide bombers killed 25 Sikhs in a temple in Kabul in Afghanistan in revenge for India's treatment of Muslims in Kashmir. The Sikhs in Afghanistan inherited the collective blame for what was going on in India. Bias due to stereotyping can affect an individual's judgement of others based on their ethnicity, gender, accent, class, religion, university education, and so on; and judgements of others can have an impact on the success or failure at job interviews or whether they are likely to be stopped and searched by the police. Such biases are often deemed implicit or unconscious and, to ensure that inadvertent discrimination does not take place, there is a perceived need to address them through some form of intervention. To support this endeavour, there are many websites and company development sessions offering 'diversity training' aimed at helping people overcome their unconscious biases, with race being the primary attribute that tests tend to measure.

There are some assumptions about cognitive biases, both in some studies by Tversky and Kahneman and among those engaged in diversity training. These include the assumption that:

- They can be measured;
- Biases are unconscious and that we respond intuitively to information that comes most immediately and automatically to mind;
- We all possess biases due to the ways our cognitive system operates;
- They form the basis of much of our attitudes and behaviour;
- Through diversity training, implicit racial bias can be reduced.

A first stage in some types of diversity training is to measure the strength of any unconscious bias a person might have. This is generally done using an implicit association test (IAT) of some kind (Greenwald, McGhee, & Schwartz, 1998) that measures latencies (slight delays) in responding to words or pictures presented on a computer. Participants might be presented with words for flowers such as 'rose' or musical instruments such as 'violin' on a computer screen and asked to respond as quickly as possible using the word 'pleasant', and to respond 'unpleasant' to insect words such as 'wasp' or weapons such as 'hatchet'. One might predict that such responses should be quite easy given the nature of the nouns and the attributes implicitly attached to them – such noun-attribute combinations are deemed compatible. There are various ways in which the instructions for this type of measure can be modified; for example, participants might be asked to reverse the associated noun-attribute so that they have to respond 'unpleasant' to 'daffodil' or 'pleasant' to 'gun'. In this case, because these combinations are assumed to be incompatible, the time taken to respond should increase compared to the compatible condition. Results from experiments by Greenwald et al. (1998) showed that significant differences in the latencies between compatible and incompatible word conditions provides evidence that we implicitly associate certain categories of things as being pleasant or unpleasant (experiment 1).

In Experiment 2, they extended this method to assessing evaluative associations between Japanese Americans and Korean Americans since each group were deemed to have negative attitudes towards the other (out-group) due to the historical occupation of Korea by the Japanese in the first half of the 20th century. The stimuli in this case were typical Japanese names and typical Korean names. As expected, the Korean American participants responded more quickly with 'pleasant' to Korean names than to Japanese names, and with a longer latency when responding 'pleasant' to Japanese names.

A third experiment looked at the patterns of attitude difference between Black (African American) and White (European American) subjects again using names typically associated with each group. In this experiment, there was a strong association between White names and 'pleasant' rather than Black names and 'pleasant'. Furthermore, the study included other measures used to compare and evaluate the IAT, the Modern Racism Scale (McConahay, Hardee, & Batts, 1981), and Diversity and Discrimination scales (Wittenbrink, Judd, & Park, 1997). Based on the answers given to these scales, the majority of the White participants had expressed no negative feelings towards African Americans, essentially a Black-White indifference, nevertheless their scores on the IAT suggested a White preference. Thus, the IAT was, arguably, tapping into unconscious bias.

WHERE DO THE BIASES COME FROM?

The biases assessed in diversity training come about because our judgements are based on the ways we have learned to categorize objects, events, and people in the past. While some stereotypes might come from personal experience, prejudice such as racism is rarely acquired that way but rather through what people learn from their sociocultural context in childhood, from their peers, and from the media. A number of cognitive social psychologists have suggested that prejudice was an inevitable outcome of such categorization processes (Beck & Forstmeier, 2007; Devine, 1989; Tajfel, 1981) and, therefore, that dealing with prejudice is likely to be difficult. As cited in Billig (1985), Tajfel (1981, p. 141) asserted that 'there is no easy way to deal with intergroup prejudice in its manifold varieties, and all one can hope for is that its more vicious and inhuman forms can be made less acute sooner or later'. Billig regarded this view as a form of fatalism, and that the categorization of a particular stimulus could be countered by *particularization* where a particular stimulus, an individual in this case, is treated as a special case. In his view, tolerance of others through this particularization process has not been sufficiently considered by the categorization psychologists. However, the argument that one can deal with implicit bias by focussing on particular cases seems to be a version of the 'no true Scotsman' fallacy where someone, who does not seem to meet all the putative criteria of a category, is considered to be not a true member of the category. The argument goes: 'No Scotsman puts sugar in his porridge.' 'But Hamish puts sugar in his porridge.' 'No *true* Scotsman puts sugar in his porridge'. Thereby, the particular case of Hamish is dismissed from the category of true Scotsmen and thus the category itself (the stereotype) lives on.

The idea that prejudice is an intractable problem continues to this day, and so, when it comes to racial, gender, educational bias, etc., there are those who argue that diversity training is ineffective. Bezrukova, Spell, Perry, & Jehn (2016) concluded that there was 'no compelling evidence that long-term effects of diversity training are sustainable in relation to attitudinal/ affective outcomes' (p. 1243). Noon (2017) questions the usefulness of applying the results of psychological tests of bias to diversity training and also argues that they are generally ineffective. He argues that it is possible that 'aversive racists' only (those who are sure they are not at all prejudiced but who have suppressed negative beliefs about racial minorities) are likely to be influenced by unconscious bias training. Measuring bias through IATs can have two potentially contradictory effects: first, to break the prejudice habit 'people must be aware of their biases and, second, they must be concerned about the consequences of their biases before they will be motivated to exert effort to eliminate them' (Devine, Forscher, Austin, and Cox 2012, p. 1268). Second, tests of bias that reveal underlying unconscious prejudice provide a way of avoiding blame since, being deeply embedded and a result of normal human categorization processes, the bias is 'not our fault'.

OVERCOMING BIASES

So, given the results of IATs, what aspects of the human cognitive system need to be addressed? Devine (1989) has referred to stereotypes as a form of habit derived from well-learned associations that are, in turn, caused by 'repeated activation in memory'. This will vary from person to person resulting in low to high levels of prejudice. Stereotyping, and hence implicit bias, is, therefore, a form of automatic and largely unconscious (heuristic) processing. According to her, when one's personal beliefs overlap with a negative stereotype, then there is the potential for explicit prejudice. Where one's personal beliefs do not overlap with the stereotype, then there is a degree of conflict since cultural stereotypes are automatically triggered for both low and high prejudiced individuals. Overcoming this habit requires conscious controlled processing. A prejudice triggered by the activation of a stereotype is the result of Type 1 thinking and is enduring and difficult to counter. On the other hand, controlled processes can cause the explicit system (Type 2 thinking) to change relatively quickly – it is 'malleable'. But, despite short-term apparent changes to expressions of explicit bias, they are likely to be short-lived.

Are there interventions that work to produce long-term changes to implicit bias; or at the very least that can mitigate the expression of bias? One way is to compare a variety of interventions to find out which ones work. Another is a scattergun approach where a range of strategies is used in a single intervention. As an example of the former strategy, Lai et al. (2014) describe an unusual research contest where a number of teams were asked to come up with various approaches that could be tested against others to see which ones, if any, reduced implicit racial preferences. The incentive for the teams of researchers who took part was to win the contest. A total of 18 interventions plus a control were used coming under the overall headings of: 'Exposure to counter-stereotypical exemplars', 'Intentional strategies to overcome biases', 'Evaluative conditioning' (in this case, pairing words: Black with positive attributes and Whites with negative attributes), 'Appeals to egalitarian values', 'Engaging with others' perspectives', and 'Inducing emotion'. Of these, the first three were effective at reducing implicit preferences and the last three ineffective. While the contest did not examine how long lasting the strategies were likely to be, the conclusion was that interventions that use multiple strategies are likely to be effective. In a follow up study, Lai et al. (2016) looked at the degree to which implicit racial preferences were reduced over time following the interventions that had shown promise. The time period over which they were tested was several hours to several days. Although the interventions showed that implicit preferences were malleable in the short term, none led to long-term change.

In contrast, an earlier study by Devine et al. (2012) claimed to produce a sustained reduction in bias over a three-month period. Their method was not to compare which method was most effective but rather to provide a variety of bias reduction strategies (five in all) in the hope that altogether they would induce a degree of self-regulation on the part of the participants. Their aim was to translate their 'situational awareness into chronic awareness of biases in themselves and in society, thereby flipping the self-regulatory switch that motivates strategy use and reduces implicit bias' (p. 1268). Based on their results, they make the case that offering a variety of strategies allows for individual differences in what is likely to motivate an individual to reduce expressions of bias by stimulating Type 2 thinking in situations that are likely to activate the (Type 1) 'habit' of bias. 'Our data provide evidence demonstrating the power of the conscious mind to intentionally deploy strategies to overcome implicit bias' (Devine et al. 2012, p. 1277).

Studies by Bruneau, Kteily, & Urbiola (2019) provide further examples of combating racial or religious bias by tapping into *collective blame hypocrisy*. This occurs when people blame an out-group (Muslims in this case) in its entirety for the bad actions of individual group members, but do not blame their own group in its entirety for bad actions by in-group members. Their method taps into our desire for consistency in our thoughts and actions. Inconsistency leads to *cognitive dissonance* with the subsequent need to remove it. An example of their studies involved US and Spanish non-Muslim students. They were given accounts of mass violence committed by white Europeans and asked, 'How responsible do you think [white Europeans/you] are for the actions of [Darren Osborne/Anders Breivik/Istvan Csontos]'. After that they were asked: 'In general, how responsible do you think white Europeans are for the attacks of white supremacists?' In the second part, the procedure was repeated but with accounts of Muslim extremists and asked: 'Fatima Wahid is a Muslim woman who owns a bakery in southern France. How responsible do you think Fatima Wahid is for the Paris attacks of 2015?' Their results showed a reduction in collective blame of Muslims both one month and one year later, particularly among those with a strong preference for consistency in their thinking.

DO MACHINES THINK DIFFERENTLY?

Instead of attempting to address these prejudicial stereotypes through some form of intervention in the hope of reducing bias against specific human groups, we could instead bypass human judgement altogether and rely instead on technology to make our assessments for us. One could, in fact, look upon this as a kind of experiment testing the hypothesis that human beings' thinking is 'faulty' in some way – we have a defective way of making assumptions about people. One possible explanation for this, as pointed out above, is that people base their judgements of other groups on what they see as specific attributes of the 'out-group' – 'they are not like us'. Whereas we would explain our own behaviour in terms of the context in which the behaviour took place ('I dropped the dish because I was in too much of a hurry'), we tend to often attribute the behaviour of others to some internal trait ('he dropped the dish because he is clumsy'). This is known as the *fundamental attribution error*. An extension of this leads to people assuming that all members of a particular group share the same attributes: 'women have no sense of direction', 'Americans are obsessed with guns', and 'people who support the Palestinians are anti-Semitic'. While this kind of error might lead to how the behaviour of particular ethnic, racial, religious, etc., groups are interpreted, there still needs to be some original source for the biased thinking in the first place.

An artificial intelligence (AI) system does not have the same cognitive system as human beings and should, therefore, be devoid of irrational prejudices and attributional biases and should rely instead on the raw data presented to it. If it is the case that humans cannot avoid biases, we should expect an AI system to make judgements free of such prejudice or bias. Typically, the form that many AI systems have used is based on a neural net where the system is trained on examples with feedback from any errors it makes. This kind of system has been used over many years in medicine. To pick but one example, doctors at Moorfields Eye Hospital in London trained an AI system to recommend treatments for 50 eye diseases. Whereas eye doctors were in agreement over 64% of the cases they viewed, the AI had 94% accuracy. If a computer system is capable of this kind of accuracy after training, the view was that an AI used, say, as a recruitment tool, would make better assessments of interview candidates than human assessors with their unconscious biases. We, therefore, have the basis of a potential experiment where the results of human assessors can be compared to the results of a computer-based system.

When Amazon piloted such a technological system as part of the recruitment process for new staff to avoid potential gender and racial stereotyping, they found that the system was dismissing female candidates for no immediately obvious reason. On examination, what had happened was that the AI was trained on past recruitment decisions that were biased in favour of men. Hence, it continued to do the same thing. Technicians then adjusted the system so that it ignored words that specified a particular gender in CVs and resumés, such as 'woman' or 'male'. However, it continued to reject female applicants based on 'implicitly gendered words' such as 'captured' or 'executed' – words that male applicants apparently used more often than females. The AI turned out to be as biased as the humans.

There are, indeed, many examples of AI systems showing systematic biases in judgement and decision-making. In the US, parts of the justice system use AI algorithms to assess the likelihood of criminals to reoffend. One system, called the Correctional Offender Management Profiling for Alternative Sanctions was analyzed by Larson, Mattu, Kirchner, & Angwin (2016). They found that it incorrectly identified black defendants as being at higher risk of reoffending than white defendants, and white defendants as being of low risk.

Bolukbasi, Chang, Zou, Saligrama, & Kalai (2016) found that Google News articles contained sexist 'word embeddings' where words like 'receptionist' were linked to 'female'. They provide a list of 'extreme she occupations' and 'extreme he occupations' that allowed the generation of analogies called proportional analogies such as she:he:: queen:king (she is to he as queen is to king). This represents an appropriate analogy. They used a machine learning algorithm to generate the endings of proportional analogies relating to jobs – she:he::?:?. When the system ran, it generated not only appropriate analogies such as the one above but inappropriate ones he:-she::computer programmer:homemaker.

'The analogies generated from these embeddings spell out the bias implicit in the data on which they were trained. Hence, word embeddings may serve as a means to extract implicit gender associations from a large text corpus similar to how Implicit Association Tests […] detect automatic gender associations possessed by people, which often do not align with self-reports' (Bolukbasi et al., 2016, p. 3).

Similarly, Kay, Matuszek, & Munson (2015) found gender biases in image searches for particular occupations. Also, in 2015, a search of images in Google for Chief Executive Officer (CEO) generated photographs of more male CEOs than female CEOs greater than the proportions in the general population, 11% vs 27% (Cossins, 2018). A cursory search by me for images of CEOs in mid 2019 showed a continuing similar disparity.

So, if humans have implicit biases, computer systems appear to have them too. The results of this virtual experiment show no differences between humans and other information processing systems (IPS). So, how do we now interpret the results given the original hypothesis that humans are somehow 'faulty' in their thinking? One view is that the biases in AI algorithms reflects human biases since the data they are trained on is biased. Hence, Richard Soccer on 17 January 2019 at the World Economic forum argued that 'Unmanaged AI is a mirror for human bias' (https://www.weforum.org/agenda/2019/01/ai-isn-t-dangerous-but-human-bias-is/). However, Karen Hao in MIT Technology Review (Hao, 2019b) points out that 'bias can creep in long before the data is collected' and at any stage: the coding stage, the collection stage, or the selection stage. In a later article she adds: 'Tech companies are built—and tech products are designed—with a "fantasy belief" that they exist independently of the sexism, racism, and societal context around them' (Hao, 2019a).

Thus, we have a chicken and egg situation. The biases come from somewhere but both AI systems and human beings are influenced by them. IPSs other than human beings are generating bias from the data they are trained on. Humans are also IPSs, so presumably we are doing the same thing. That is, our biases are due to being trained on the data through the environment and sociocultural influences we are exposed to. The environment, including the social environment, influences human activity and ways of thinking. At the same time, human activity and thought have an effect on the environment. We can therefore end up with a positive feedback loop whereby a particular opinion (or 'meme' in the original Dawkins (1976) sense), for example, is noticed and shared which causes it to be noticed by more people and shared, and so on. This way a particular political or social view can gain currency, and we can track the rise of social movements as they increase in influence. These can be either positive or negative. Historically, there has been the rise of Nazism in Germany or Mao Zedong in China, the abolitionists in the UK and the US, the suffragette movement, white supremacist terrorism, the MeToo movement, and so on. These days such feedback loops are amplified by the 'echo chamber' provided by social media, but more importantly they show that aspects of our culture can be changed. Our thinking is the product of the culture we are immersed in. We learn about ethics, morality, technology, stereotypes, and all the rest whether we want to or not. According to Hinton (2017a, 2017b), if it is our determination to counter implicit sexism, racism, elitism, etc. and, given it is difficult to change our minds, we should concentrate on changing our culture since the bias is in the data.

SUMMARY

We often rely on stereotypes to make judgements about people from a particular social group since they are deemed to inherit the attributes of that group. Hasty induction can mean that the attributes of an individual from an unfamiliar group is assumed to be representative of the group. Such stereotypes can lead to potential biases against people's ethnicity, gender, accent, class, religion, university education, and so on.

The IAT has been used to elicit unconscious bias and diversity training has been established by firms and institutions to attempt to counter or make people aware of such implicit bias.

Stereotypes and associated biases are deemed by many to arise from normal categorization processes. According to some researchers, this can cause diversity training to be ineffective or short lived. A variety of bias reduction strategies may work by catering for individual differences among people. Collective blame is often ascribed to an out-group due to the actions of a small minority and can be reduced by pointing out the hypocrisy and inconsistency involved, as collective blame is not directed at the in-group.

AI systems have been found to exhibit bias as they have been trained on data produced by people. It can be argued that people also are 'trained' on the same data. Rather than fixing the cognitive system, it would be more effective to change the culture that gives rise to the bias in the first place.

SUGGESTED FURTHER READING

Devine, P. G., Forscher, P. S., Austin, A. J., & Cox, W. T. (2012, Nov). Long-term reduction in implicit race bias: A prejudice habit-breaking intervention. *Journal of Experimental Social Psychology*, *48*(6), 1267–1278. Retrieved from https://doi.org/10.1016/j.jesp.2012.06.003

Hinton, P. (2017). *Stereotypes and the construction of the social world.* London, UK: Routledge.

Payne, K., Niemi, L., & Doris, J. M. (2018). *How to think about "implicit bias" Scientific American.*

7

THE CONFABULATING MIND

INTRODUCTION

As we have seen, we don't always manage to think things through as if we were perfectly rational creatures with immense memories, so our thoughts and decisions often rely on heuristics which, in turn, may be generated by influences that we are only vaguely aware of. Our actions are, therefore, the outcome of wherever our thoughts have been buffeted by those influences. Decisions can end up being made depending on what associations comes to mind most quickly, what something looks like or sounds like, how important the decision is, what a pop/film/football star does, and so on. This can be particularly relevant when a person, group or company is attempting to persuade us to do something.

HOW TO MAKE PEOPLE AN OFFER THEY CAN'T REFUSE

There are many techniques of persuasion that rely on us not considering things in any great depth. One theory to explain what goes on is the *elaboration likelihood model* of persuasion put forward by Petty and Cacioppo (1984). They argued that there are two routes to persuasion: a carefully considered one, a *central route*, and a *peripheral route* where persuasion takes place depending on such things as how you are feeling, whether a celebrity had endorsed a product, or the wording of an ad. For example, a product that is 90% fat free would be considered more persuasive than one that advertised itself as 10% fat. One emphasizes the lack of fat and the other its presence (Levin & Gaeth, 1988; Tversky & Kahneman, 1981). Similarly, hearing that you have a 2% chance of developing breast cancer over the next five years sounds more frightening than being told that you have a 98% chance of not developing it. Statements such as 'up to 50% off!' includes zero but zero is not what is being emphasized. In the past, a scantily clad model draped over a car has been shown to influence people's (well, mainly men's) estimate of how fast the car was. When you have the time and the motivation to elaborate on what you are being told about a product, then you would be going down the central route.

A common feature of some forms of persuasion is stating something that doesn't actually mean anything in the hope that the reader is not paying enough attention to notice, such as the 'Persil washes whiter' ad from 1955. The statement doesn't say what it washes whiter than. This kind of ad uses a 'hanging comparative' where whatever it seems to be comparing itself to is not mentioned.

'IBM makes storage easier, cheaper and greener.
IBM promises tools for better storage and improved energy consumption'

Easier than what? Cheaper than what? Improved compared to what?

Another example comes from the Feedback section in New Scientist from 2004 where a reader submitted this ad: 'Pears Herbal Care Aloe Vera, Honeysuckle and Vitamin E Shampoo maintains the health and shine of normal hair for less than the more expensive brands'. Presumably, it also does so for more than the less expensive brands, or for the same as brands that are the same price. In cases such as these, and they are ubiquitous, the advertisers are trying to influence your behaviour through the shallow peripheral route (mainly Type 1) in the hope that you won't use the deeper central processing route (Type 2) or you would realize they are meaningless. These are not exactly subtle messages but their impact on our choices can be.

MISTAKING IMPLICATIONS FOR ASSERTIONS

Before the Battle of Pteria in 547BCE, the Lydian king Croesus sought the advice of the oracle at Delphi. The oracle is reported to have replied that, 'if King Croesus crosses the Halys River, a great empire will be destroyed'. Croesus mistook the implication for an assertion that he would destroy the Persian empire but it was his own great empire that was destroyed. Pragmatic implications are 'statements that lead a person to believe something that is neither explicitly stated nor necessarily implied' (Searleman & Carter, 1988, p. 265). The reason such techniques of persuasion work is because we are very good at making inferences and assumptions. This is sensible since we spend much of our time filling in the gaps in the partial information that come through our senses. If someone at a dinner table asks, 'Is there any salt?' the answer 'Yes' is not the appropriate response (see Chapter 1). The pragmatic implication is that the person is asking for someone to pass the salt. In situations such as the one King Croesus found himself in, one can mistake implications for assertions and there are cases where it is important to distinguish between them such as a courtroom testimony. Harris, Teske, and Ginn (1975) presented people with two versions of statements from a five-minute mock trial testimony. In one version, participants heard: 'that absent-minded Herman lost his walkie-talkie too' and 'I walked away without taking any money'. In another, these were changed to: 'that absent-minded Herman didn't have his walkie-talkie either,' and 'I was able to walk away without taking any money.' In the second case, the statement that the speaker was able to walk away only pragmatically implies that he did in fact walk away. There were 18 versions of such statements and participants were asked 36 true or false questions. Participants were divided into two groups:

one group was given instructions similar to the ones given in a real courtroom; another group were given specific instructions to distinguish between assertions and implications. However, there were no significant differences between the groups when asked the true/false questions suggesting that they were unable to distinguish between a pragmatic implication and an assertion.

Searleman and Carter (1988) performed an experiment using taped commercials about fictitious products. They looked at the pragmatic implications based on juxtaposition: 'Get a goodnight's sleep. Buy Dreamon Sleeping Pills.' The juxtaposition implies that the pills will help you sleep but it doesn't actually say that. Another is based on hedge words such as 'Ty-One-On pain reliever may help get rid of these morning after headaches' where 'may' indicates a weak assertion but a strong implication (p. 266). Participants were presented with either versions involving a pragmatic implication and ones involving an assertion: 'Ty-One-On pills will cure morning after headaches.' After a five-minute delay, there was no significant difference between True responses for implied versus asserted statements, although there was a significant difference for the ones that were tested immediately. Versions using hanging comparatives were the least successful at misleading participants. However, these results were for participants taking part in an experiment and who were being tested subsequently. When ads appear on billboards, Facebook, TV, radio, etc., we don't expect to be tested on them and hence are even more likely to mistake implications for assertions.

THE RHYME AS REASON EFFECT (AKA THE KEATS EFFECT)

There are other techniques that can have a subtle effect on persuasion. In a study in 2000, rejoicing in the title of 'Birds of a Feather Flock Conjointly', on the effect of aphorisms on people's perception of their accuracy, McGlone and Tofighbakhsh (2000) found that unfamiliar rhyming aphorisms such as, 'What sobriety conceals, alcohol reveals' were judged to be more accurate than versions that did not rhyme such as, 'What sobriety conceals, alcohol unmasks'. This is an example of the *rhyme as reason effect* where the use of poetic devices makes people feel that the statement is somehow true or accurate, hence the alternative name of the *Keats effect*. So, an assertion such as 'Beauty is Truth and Truth Beauty, – That is all/Ye know on earth and all ye need to know' sounds so … true. Until you start to examine it and decide that there are probably other things ye need to know.

Poetic phrases, therefore, work subliminally, or peripherally. The UK Conservative Party seem to be better versed (to maintain the metaphor) than other UK parties and know the value of alliteration and repetition. Thus, in the run-up to the 2017 general election, we heard that the Conservatives represented 'strong and stable' government unlike the 'coalition of chaos' that other parties represented. There is, of course, a danger that aphorisms can be repeated too much, so some news media eventually start reporting the number of times a cliché is mentioned in a speech so they begin to lose their impact: 'Brexit means Brexit' – That is all ye know on earth and all ye need to know.

CHOOSING COMPETENT POLITICIANS THE EASY WAY

Our senses are continually being bombarded by information from all around us and most of the time, we are very good at filtering it to extract the useful bits. To do this, we can rely on salient superficial features in the natural world, usually unconsciously. For example, if a fruit is red, then it's probably ripe. If a creature has feathers, flies, and sings, then it almost certainly lays eggs. This is Type 1 in operation. However, when it comes to something more important such as who to vote for in an election, one might expect Type 2 to kick in. For example, we might consider various factors such as the policies of the candidate, the candidate's probity, or how much money has been spent on the campaign. Essentially, we at least want someone who is competent. Or who looks competent. In fact, looking at someone's face for a few seconds, or even milliseconds, might be enough. Todorov, Mandisodza, Goren, and Hall (2005) decided to see if there were heuristics people used to judge competence. They asked approximately a thousand people to rate photographs of people in terms of how competent they looked. What their participants didn't realize was that they were looking at photographs of candidates for the US Senate and House of Representatives in three elections. People's judgements of whether someone looked competent correlated significantly with the actual election results. People picked candidates who were actually elected 66% to 73% of the time. They got the same results by asking people to look at a photo for just one second. Todorov et al. (2005) concluded that people's voting behaviour was likely to be influenced by an unconscious, initial, and intuitive reaction to what the candidate looked like.

In a follow-up series of experiments, Ballew and Todorov (2007) presented the photographs of 89 (unfamiliar) candidates for gubernatorial elections in the United States and again asked participants to judge which one they thought looked the most competent. In different conditions, participants were presented with the photographs for either 100 milliseconds, 250 milliseconds or until the participant made a choice. Even after only 100 milliseconds exposure, participants chose the winning candidate better than chance. In a second experiment, participants were asked to deliberate and think carefully before choosing rather than rely on 'gut feelings'. Perhaps surprisingly, performance in the deliberate condition was poorer than in the 100 millisecond and 25 millisecond conditions. The 'competent looking face' was an effective heuristic in choosing who might win an election. Their final experiment involved collecting competence judgements before the 2006 election. Once again, these judgements predicted 68.6% of the gubernatorial election results and 72.4% of the Senate ones. The results can be interpreted as evidence for a peripheral route appearing to influence voting choices more than the central route. It also suggests that people in general may be choosing to vote for candidates based largely on superficial features. This suggests a further question: to what extent are we consciously aware of the reasons for our choices?

HOW DO WE JUSTIFY OUR CHOICES?

What are we thinking when we choose a dress, a film to watch, a meal in a restaurant? When we make such a choice, what evaluations are we making and how accurate are our introspections into our thinking? In a paper in 1977, Nisbett and Wilson discussed a wide range of studies where participants seemed to be incapable of reporting their own cognitive processes accurately. In the studies they mentioned, researchers would manipulate some aspects of the experiment to see how the participants would react and also what they said about the causes of their behaviour. In a study by Maier (1931), participants were asked to tie two strings together that were suspended from the ceiling. Unfortunately, they couldn't reach both strings at the same time. During the experiment, Maier 'accidentally' brushed against a string causing it to swing. This, in turn, provided a hint to the participants that they could cause the string to swing and then grab it while holding onto the other one. When asked what gave them the idea of causing the string to swing, none mentioned the accidental hint Maier had given. In studies by Latané and Darley (1970) on the bystander effect, participants' behaviour changed depending on whether other people were present. When asked about their behaviour, they did not claim that the presence of others had anything to do with it. Storms and Nisbett (1970) gave participants a placebo pill they claimed caused either arousal or relaxation to different groups of insomnia sufferers. They, like the participants in the other experiments, gave reasons for their change in behaviour or attitude that had nothing to do with the manipulations being tested.

In one often quoted experiment, Nisbett and Wilson (1977) asked passers-by in clothing stores to evaluate certain articles of clothing. Some subjects were shown four different nightgowns and others four identical pairs of stockings and asked to say which was the best quality, and once they had done that, they were asked why they had chosen it. They found that there was a left-to-right position effect with marked preference for choosing the rightmost article, particularly when presented with the identical stockings. When asked why they had chosen it, people gave various reasons that had nothing to do with the position of the garment. 'And, when asked directly about a possible effect of the position of the article, virtually all subjects denied it, usually with a worried glance at the interviewer suggesting that they felt either that they had misunderstood the question or were dealing with a madman' (p. 244). Based on the research, they discuss as well as their own studies, Nisbett and Wilson argue that people do not have sufficient access to the processes by which their decisions were made but instead generated explanations based on *a priori* personal and cultural beliefs including stereotypes (the representativeness heuristic).

There have been criticisms of the Nisbett and Wilson's experiments but relatively little in the way of follow-up studies since then. White (1980) has argued that the reason people are unable to provide an accurate account of the process by which an evaluation of judgement was made is because of the 'distance' between the process and the subsequent report. White (1987) also argued that the assumption of a relationship between 'introspective access' and subsequent report accuracy is problematic.

These results suggest that our behaviour and the mental representation of that behaviour are somehow at odds. Chapter 1 introduced the idea that we can mentally represent the world so that we can make plans, predict outcomes, and act accordingly. If the outcome matches the intention, then that's fine. If not, then we would need to adapt our behaviour both to deal with the new outcome and to update our knowledge so that we can plan more accurately in the future. Johansson, Hall, Sikström, and Olsson (2005) wanted to find out what would happen if that intention-outcome loop was disrupted without the person being aware of the disruption. The experimenter held two photographs (A and B) of women, one in each hand, and the participant was asked to choose which one in their opinion was the more attractive. In one (manipulated) condition, the experimenter used a sleight of hand technique. Although each hand showed a photograph – e.g., photo A in his right hand and photo B in his left – he also concealed a copy of photo B behind photo A and a copy of photo A behind photo B in his left. Having shown both photographs, the experimenter then put them face down on the table and asked the participant to choose. If the participant chose A from the experimenter's right hand, then the experimenter actually passed him photo B face down while hiding photo A under his sleeve. The participant was asked to look at the photo and give a reason for choosing that photo. Participants in the non-manipulated condition, where the photos where not switched, were also asked why they had chosen it.

While about 26% of the participants detected that a switch had been made in the manipulated condition, most did not and provided a reason for the 'choice' even though it was not the choice they had originally made. Johansson et al. categorized the reasons given under the headings *emotionality* – they assumed there would be less emotional engagement with the wrong photo; *specificity* – participants' reports would be less specific and detailed; and *certainty* – they may show evidence of being less sure about their response. However, since it turned out that there was no significant difference in the kinds of reasons people gave in the manipulated (M) and non-manipulated (NM) conditions, participants may simply have been confabulating in both – they were making their reasons up. Much like the participants in Nisbett and Wilson's studies, they were giving *post hoc* rationalizations for their choice. Johansson et al. referred to this phenomenon in the M condition as *choice blindness* in analogy to change blindness (see Chapter 1).

In follow-up studies, Johansson, Hall, Sikstrom, Tarning, and Lind (2006) analyzed the responses given in both M and NM conditions in terms of their linguistic content. Again, it appeared that, not only did participants offer confabulatory explanations for the choices they had not made, but also that participants may well have offered the same kind of confabulatory explanations for the choices they actually did make.

In a further study in 2018, Strandberg, Sivén, Hall, Johansson, and Pärnamets (2018) found that the manipulation of the faces in a partial replication of the Johansson et al's (2005) study caused people to subsequently rate the originally rejected face as more attractive thus their evaluations had been altered by the methodology of the study rather than by any other objective criterion.

It's one thing to alter people's perceptions of faces without them being aware of it, it's another to alter one's decisions or views about something more important such as moral values or political affiliations. So, if we make a decision, is it really the case that the reasons we give for that decision are just made up as we go along? And if we don't always know why we really choose to do something, to what extent can we be said to be in control of our own actions?

SO, WHO DO YOU THINK YOU ARE?

When giving reasons for our choices, we are prone, it appears, to confabulating. When we think about what kind of person we ourselves are, are we also confabulating? Research has shown that we do not always make realistic assessments of our own personality traits, strengths, weaknesses, and knowledge. For example, Donald Trump has said on several occasions how very humble he is. The very assertion negates the trait he ascribes to himself and for which there is no evidence. Two related biases are known as *belief superiority* where people believe that their own beliefs are superior to or more accurate than those of others, and *illusory superiority,* or the 'better-than-average effect (BTAE)', where the majority of people in a particular category believe they are better than the average of their peers (other students, other drivers, other teachers, and so on). The BTAE would appear to be a fundamental aspect of human psychology. Like many biases, there is a very good reason why we have developed them over the course of evolution. In this case, unrealistic positivity can instil confidence, motivation, and perseverance. Feeling good about ourselves when we compare ourselves to others is better than feeling inferior. Obviously, people would not perform well or might suffer from depression if they thought that they were worse than everyone else or that other people were superior to them. Indeed, there is evidence that some people in important positions feel like a 'fraud', a feeling of illusory inferiority. This is the *imposter syndrome*, first described by Pauline Clance among high-achieving women (Clance & O'Toole, 1987; Sakulku & Alexander, 2011), although the phenomenon applies equally to men (Bothello & Roulet, 2019), and can, indeed, lead to feelings of stress and anxiety.

One downside of the illusory superiority effect is that people are liable to blame external forces for failures and ascribe successes to internal processes. Another is that by refusing to acknowledge where their competences fail them, they are unlikely to rectify any faults or areas of ignorance they may have. When it comes to knowledge and expertise rather than personality traits, there is a cognitive bias known as the *Dunning-Kruger effect* where people who have a relatively low level of competence in an area tend to regard themselves as more competent than they actually are. Those with a high level of competence, however, tend to underestimate their competence. Kruger and Dunning (1999) performed a number of studies to examine differences between those deemed 'competent' in a particular field and those deemed 'incompetent' in terms of their ability to recognize their own competence. They considered four hypotheses: the first was that incompetent performers would tend to overestimate their abilities compared to competent performers using objective criteria. Indeed, they predicted that those in the bottom quarter of the distribution would be unaware that they had performed poorly. Awareness of and ability to assess one's own cognitive skills is known as *metacognition*. So, a second hypothesis was that incompetent people would show a deficit in metacognitive skills compared to competent individuals. A third prediction related to an inability among incompetent individuals to use the performance of others to assess their own ability and performance. They used a range of topic areas such as humour, logical reasoning, and knowledge of English grammar. The various tests of the first three hypotheses showed that those on the bottom quartile of the distributions did indeed overestimate their abilities compared to their actual results. Those in the top quartile generally underestimated theirs.

A fourth prediction was that if the performance of incompetents could be improved only then would their metacognitive skills also improve. That is, participants would show a more accurate assessment of their ability and would be more accurate in assessing their test score.

> 'If ... it takes competence to recognize competence, then manipulating competence ought to enable the incompetent to recognize that they have performed poorly. Of course, there is a paradox to this assertion. It suggests that the way to make incompetent individuals realize their own incompetence is to make them competent' (Kruger & Dunning, 1999, p. 1128).

The results of training on logical reasoning problems resulted in significant shifts in their metacognitive skills (although they were still prone to overestimate their ability and performance) and more accurate assessment of their test score. Competent individuals tended to underestimate their ability possibly because they assumed their peers were at least as good as them.

Alicke, Klotz, Breitenbecher, Yurak, and Vredenburg (1995) pointed out that the BTAE is affected by the type of dimension being compared. Some traits can be objectively measured such as abilities (intellectual, musical, mathematical, etc.), others are vaguer or more ambiguous such as emotional traits like generosity, kindness, honesty, etc. Many of these studies are conducted on college students and many ask the students to compare themselves to the average student. Alicke et al. (1995) therefore wanted to find out what the difference would be if participants were to either compare themselves to the average student or compare themselves to a particular unfamiliar student. They used a 9-point scale to ask the students to compare themselves with the average student using a rating scale from 'much less than the average college student' to 'much more than the average college student' on 20 positive traits (e.g., considerate, polite, co-operative, friendly, and responsible) and

20 negative traits (e.g., meddlesome, lazy, vain, and disrespectful). In another condition, participants were seated next to another student of the same sex they did not know who was then moved to another seat further away before the study began. The same traits were used and the same rating scale, but the question asked them to compare themselves to 'the person you were sitting next to'. The results showed that the BTAE was larger for participants who compared themselves with an average college student rather than a specific one even though they were not known to the participant.

Sedikides, Meek, Alicke, and Taylor (2014) decided to test the BTAE by examining the views of a group that one would not normally consider average in terms of desirable characteristics. Furthermore, they sought some kind of objective standard that would allow them to measure the BTAE against. Indeed, by assessing prisoners incarcerated for a variety of crimes, they sought to assess the extent of the BTAE given the prisoners' objectively low status on a number of traits – whether they were more honest, moral, dependable, law-abiding, and so on – compared to other prisoners or the non-incarcerated community at large. What they found was that, compared to other prisoners, the participants saw themselves as significantly 'more moral, kinder to others, more self-controlled, more law-abiding, more compassionate, more generous, more dependable, more trustworthy, and more honest' (p. 399). Their view of the future was the same as that of non-incarcerated people in that they saw their future in a much better light than their past. For example, they felt they were less likely to commit further crimes in the future despite the actual rate of recidivism showing that this was unlikely. Perhaps surprisingly, they also rated themselves significantly higher on all traits except law-abidingness than the community outside prison. Despite the fact that they had been found guilty of a crime and sentenced to prison, they saw themselves as being as law-abiding as the general population. While the results might suggest that the prisoners are in denial about their crimes, their responses are no different from other groups that Kruger and

Dunning (1999, p. 401) regard as occupying 'the unfavourable end of ability distributions'.

CAUSAL ATTRIBUTIONS

The reasons we give for the outcome of events often depends on the nature of the event. For example, if you do well in an exam to what do you ascribe your success? Is it because of your hard work, intelligence, or luck? Was it perhaps simply an easy exam? If you do badly is it because you didn't work hard enough or because you're not clever enough? Were there questions you weren't expecting, or ones the lecturer didn't cover?

People vary in the causal attributions they make depending on the outcome of events. We often tend to make external attributions for our failures or errors and internal ones for our successes. If we do well in the exam, it's because we worked hard or we're just clever – an internal attribution. If we do badly, then it's due to something to do with the exam not us – an external attribution. The fact that people's explanations for their actions can be dubious is important in a number of fields. In criminological psychology, for example, attention is generally paid to the reasons criminals give for their actions so that those reasons can be understood and action taken based on them. Typically, they explain their offending as being due to some external cause rather than due to something within themselves. However, in studies of criminal behaviour, it is quite possible that the explanations offenders give for their offending might not bear any relation to the real reasons for the offence. 'In almost every such study, it is found that people will seek to excuse these behaviours by seeking out external, unstable and specific causes, rather than internalizing personal responsibility. In other words, when we humans do bad things, we typically say, "But it wasn't my fault"!' (Maruna & Mann, 2006, p. 156). According to Maruna and Mann, there is a belief that the excuses that offenders give precede the offence. In other words, it is the situation the offender finds him or herself in that gives rise to the offence: 'He was in my way,' 'She was wearing a short skirt,' 'I was drunk'. Furthermore, excuses and justifications are regarded as ways of avoiding responsibility, the implication being that law-abiding citizens don't do that kind of thing. 'Yet, the psychological literature on excuse making is clear that taking full responsibility for every personal failing does not make a person normal, it makes them extraordinary – and possibly at risk of mental illness' (p. 162). As a result, Maruna and Mann (2006, p. 158) argue that: 'criminological psychology may be guilty of committing something akin to the "fundamental attribution error" […] writ large'.

Evans (2017) argues that the idea that we are capable of explaining our behaviour is an example of folk psychology. He points out that opinion pollsters are guilty of this when they ask people why they intend to vote in a particular way. However, 'one of the basic rules of psychology is that people will answer any damn silly question you put to them. That does not mean you should believe the answers' (p. 12). In his book, 'The Mind Is Flat', Nick Chater takes an even stronger view: 'There is no inner world. Our flow of momentary conscious experience is not the sparkling surface of at vast sea of thought – it is all there is' (Chater, 2018, p. 8). In a section on The Illusion Of Explanatory Depth, he argues that:

> 'Chess grandmasters, it turns out, can't really explain how they play chess; doctors can't explain how they diagnose patients; none of us can remotely explain how we understand the everyday world of people and objects. What we say sounds like an explanation – but really it is a terrible jumble that we are making up as we go along' (p. 28).

SUMMARY

Our thinking can be influenced by the way information is framed. It is possible to persuade people to make decisions based on a peripheral route (via Type 1 thinking) on the assumption that they will avoid the central processing route (Type 2 thinking). We are very good at making assumptions on flimsy evidence, such as pragmatic implications, which can often be very useful but can lead to mistaken inferences. Alliteration and rhyme can have a greater impact in persuasion than prosaic statements (the 'Keats effect').

Judgements of a politician's competence can rely on superficial features such as what someone looks like rather than an analysis of policies or history (see also Chapter 8 'Confirmation Bias Revisited'). Furthermore, there is evidence that we tend to confabulate when we try to justify or explain our actions or choices.

We are even prone to confabulating when we assess our own strengths and weaknesses. The BTAE, or the illusory superiority effect, refers to a bias whereby a majority of people feel they are better than average. There is also the imposter syndrome where some high achieving people feel that they are frauds.

When we perform an action leading to an outcome, the success of that outcome can be ascribed to either internal causes or external ones. In a prison study, some offenders attributed their offending on external factors influencing them rather than internal ones. While they are being judged for not taking responsibility for their actions, they are not doing anything other than what most of us do.

The fact that we are sometimes poor at explaining our behaviour is known as the 'illusion of explanatory depth'. We make up explanations as we go along.

SUGGESTED FURTHER READING

Chater, N. (2018). *The mind is flat*. London, UK: Allen Lane.

Nisbett, R. E., & Wilson, T. D. (1977). Telling more than we can know: Verbal reports on mental processes. *Psychological Review*, *84*, 231–259.

PART 4
MOTIVATED COGNITION

8

MISTAKEN BELIEFS ABOUT THE WORLD

NAÏVE PHYSICS

You come home on a cold winter's evening to find that your house does not feel warm enough. You have a heating system controlled by a thermostat. What do you do to get warmer? Some people might turn up the thermostat, others might put on a warm jersey. Now, imagine that the thermostat is set at 21 degrees centigrade. The temperature outside the house is below freezing. If you are cold, that would suggest that the heating system is unable to reach 21 degrees. If the temperature cannot reach 21 degrees, then turning the thermostat up to 23 degrees will have no effect since it is not going to reach 23 degrees either. What you end up doing is based on whatever mental model you have of the heating system, and for many of us, this may be based on naive beliefs of some physical systems.

Kempton (1986) argued that people have 'folk theories' about such systems. He showed evidence that people had either a 'valve theory' or a 'feedback theory' of how thermostats work.

The model people had of a thermostat under the valve theory was analogous to a valve in a water pipe. If not enough water is coming through, then open the valve further and more will come out. This is, however, an incorrect model of how a basic thermostat works. It doesn't increase or decrease the amount of heat that comes out, it is simply an on-off switch. (It has been argued that a thermostat has two beliefs: 'it's not warm enough: switch on' and 'It's too warm: switch off'. See Thagard, 2014). The feedback model is better related to how a thermostat works. For example, one of Kempton's interviewees stated: 'You just turn the thermostat up, and once she [sic] gets up there [to the desired temperature] she'll kick off automatically. And then she'll kick on and off to keep it at that temperature' (p. 80).

A follow-up study of mental models of home heating was conducted by Revell and Stanton (2014). They looked at a much more complicated model of home heating involving the various systems used in the house: gas supply, water supply, boiler (furnace), radiators, boiler control panel, thermostat, etc. They also found valve and feedback mental models being used to understand and interact with the thermostat, as well as other models of the heating system as an 'integrated set of control devices'. For physical systems, the designer of a device such as a smartphone, or system such as a heating system, has a mental model of how the device should operate. The device itself presents some kind of interface to the user (controls, buttons, computer screen, etc.). Based on the device interface, the user generates their own mental model that may be different from what the designer expected. Three of Revell and Stanton's six participants, for example, had mental models that differed significantly from how the heating system actually worked.

People can have mental models of any number of systems both physical and abstract. Chapter 2 has briefly discussed the idea of 'folk physics'. These are models of how the world works some of which appear to be innate. Yet, despite familiarity with kicking footballs, dropping things, spinning things, and letting them go for dogs to chase, and so on, we can often be unsure of what path the object takes when kicked or dropped or thrown. Box 8.1 has a couple of examples of problems involving motion.

BOX 8.1 LAWS OF MOTION

In Figure 8.1, someone throws a ball into the air. What force is acting on it at A as it rises and what acts on it at B?
Someone holds a high velocity rifle aimed horizontally. A bullet is fired from the rifle and at exactly the same time a bullet is dropped to the ground from the same height as the rifle bullet. Which one hits the ground first?

McCloskey, Caramazza, and Green (1980) wanted to find out what kinds of mental models people with varying degrees of expertise of physics had about simple physical systems. They presented participants with diagrams of curved tubes or of someone swinging a metal ball at high speed above their head. For the curved tubes, they were told that a ball enters at one point and shoots out of the other end (see Figure 8.2). The task was to draw the path the ball would take when it leaves the tube. For the swinging metal ball (see Figure 8.3), they were asked to draw the path the ball would take if it was let go at a particular point. In part (a) in Figure 8.2, two-thirds of

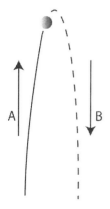

FIGURE 8.1 Path of a ball thrown into the air.

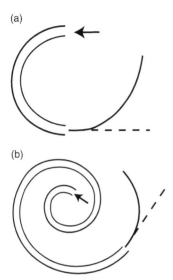

FIGURE 8.2 Examples of figures similar to those used in McCloskey et al.'s studies. A ball enters at the position of the arrow in both figures. Participants are asked to draw the path the ball takes when it shoots out of the curved tubes. These are represented by the solid (curved) lines in the figures. The correct path is shown by the dotted line.

respondents were correct in identifying the straight line path the ball would take on leaving the curved tube (the dotted lines), with one-third drawing a curved path. However, in part (b), more than half assumed the ball would take a curved path. For the spinning ball in Figure 8.3, only slightly more than half indicated the correct path the ball would take. Even some students who had completed physics courses showed evidence of having erroneous laws of motion.

McCloskey (1983, p. 299) argued that naive models of motion were 'remarkably similar to a pre-Newtonian physical theory popular in the fourteenth through sixteenth centuries'. That is, the mental model people have about moving objects has been attributed to a belief in an 'impetus theory'. Impetus is a kind of force that is acquired from the action of another

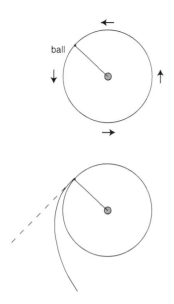

FIGURE 8.3 People were presented with the diagram at the top of the figure representing someone spinning a ball on a string above their head. Participants were asked to draw the path of the ball if the string breaks at the point where the ball is in the figure. Slightly over half chose the correct (dotted) path; 30% drew a curved path with a small number drawing other paths.

object such as a hand throwing a ball. This force is passed to the ball and causes it to maintain its motion. According to McCloskey (1983), a folk theory of motion is based on everyday experience, although with some individual differences, and is incompatible with physical principles. Furthermore, the folk theories seem to remain even after physics training. Regarding the faulty model as a theory sounds as if people are consciously applying it, whereas they may simply be relying on their memory of previous experiences. Hence, Kozhevnikov and Hegarty (2001) refer to people using a heuristic rather than a theory. Meanwhile, White (2009) regards this passing of a force as an example of the 'tendency for the causal object to impose its own properties on the effect object'. For example, 'someone grasps and lifts an object. Part of what is involved in that causal relation is that the kinematic properties [the direction of motion] of the actor's hand are imposed on the object' (p. 774). Whichever view one takes, the point is that many people mistakenly see the force acting at point A in Figure 8.1 as something that has been transferred to the ball by the action of the hand causing it to continue to rise. Similarly, the rifle produces a force on the bullet that causes it to continue its motion. In both cases, however, the only force acting on the ball or the bullet is gravity.

Hecht and Bertamini (2000) showed participants a number of diagrams showing a stick figure throwing a ball to another stick figure. These included a semi-circular path, a parabola, a straight line with a vertical drop at the end, a deformed parabola that turns down towards the end of the trajectory, amongst others. People were asked to indicate which path was the most realistic. They were also asked to indicate on a trajectory divided into several sections, where they though the ball was moving fastest. Somewhat to the surprise of the investigators, the point at which people indicated that the ball was moving fastest was at some point after it had left the thrower's hand, often at the apex of its trajectory. In other words, it seemed to have accelerated after leaving the thrower's hand.

In other more abstract domains, faulty mental models can be dangerous. For example, Meyer (2010) has pointed out that people can have faulty mental models of the damage caused by disasters. People tend to misrepresent the future consequences of not evacuating when a hurricane, flood, or forest fire approaches. Faulty mental models of climate change can have disastrous effects for the entire planet. In a study published in 2007 (but carried out several years earlier), Sterman and Sweeney (2007) reported studies on highly educated MIT graduate students about their understanding of climate dynamics. They found that their mental model of the effects of greenhouse gas emissions caused many of them to favour a wait-and-see policy (much like many politicians):

'Atmospheric CO_2 keeps rising even as emissions fall – as long as emissions exceed removal. Because emissions are now roughly double net removal, stabilizing emissions near current rates will lead to continued increases in atmospheric CO_2. In contrast, most subjects believe atmospheric CO_2 can be stabilized by stabilizing emissions at or above current rates, and while emissions continuously exceed removal. Such beliefs – analogous to arguing a bathtub filled faster than it drains will never overflow – support wait-and-see policies, but violate basic laws of physics' (p. 236).

Or as Bayne (2013) puts it: 'beliefs have consequences, and false beliefs can have disastrous consequences' (see also Chapter 9).

Confirmation bias leads to what Flynn, Nyhan, and Reifler (2017) refer to as 'directionally motivated reasoning' which is reasoning motivated by one's goals. This can be at the expense of accuracy since goals can distort the choice and evaluation of evidence if they don't fit with our goals (Epley & Gilovich, 2016). Directionally motivated reasoning, therefore, involves both confirmation bias and disconfirmation bias in that it leads people to notice or seek out information that reinforces pre-existing attitudes and dismiss and argue against information that contradicts them. As a result, people will find information that backs up their views as more convincing than contrary information.

'WHEN PROPHECY FAILS'

What, then, do we do when there is incontrovertible information that contradicts what we believe to be true? Well, obviously what we should do is to disregard what we once believed and embrace the new evidence. Except that we find it very hard to do that. One reason for this is that the contradiction between our beliefs and our behaviour causes what psychologist Festinger (1957) called cognitive dissonance. Because of this inconsistency or potential inconsistency between our attitudes and our behavior, something has to give. Often this means reinterpreting our behaviour to remove the inconsistency so they still fit with our attitudes, which Festinger referred to as eliminating the dissonance between them.

To test this idea, Festinger and Carlsmith (1959) ran an experiment in which 3 groups of 20 people were asked to perform a boring task for a monetary reward. They then had to tell someone else (a confederate of the experimenter) that the task was actually exciting. One of the groups was paid a small amount for their participation ($ 1), another was paid a rather large amount ($ 20 – a considerable amount in 1957), and a control group were not paid. Finally, both groups were asked to rate how much they enjoyed the task. Cognitive dissonance theory predicted that the group that was paid $ 1 would feel greater dissonance between their self-esteem and the fact that they were paid little to carry out a boring task, and between their self-esteem and lying to someone about how exciting it was. To eliminate the dissonance, Festinger and Carlsmith predicted that they would reinterpret their actions and hence rate the boring task as more exciting than the $ 20 group who were paid enough money to lie about it, so they felt no such dissonance.

The participants were asked 4 questions using an 11-point scale from –5 to +5. These were as follows:

- Were the tasks interesting and enjoyable?
- Did you get an opportunity to learn about your own ability?
- Were they measuring anything important?
- Would you take part in a similar experiment?

The only question to produce significant differences between the groups was the question about how exciting it was. Here the Control group scored an average of –.45; the $ 1 group scored +1.35; and the $ 20 group scored –.05. In case anyone wonders how the experimenters could afford to give $ 20 to the participants given that it would be equivalent to over $ 220 today (so the equivalent of $ 4,400 for the $ 20 group alone), they were actually asked to return the money at the end of the experiment after an explanation of what the experiment was really about. Which they did.

A more dramatic real-world study took place in 1954 when a charismatic housewife, to whom Festinger and colleagues

(Festinger et al. 1956/2008) gave the pseudonym Marian Keech, convinced a group of followers that she had received a message from the planet Clarion stating that the world would end in a great flood before sunrise on 21 December 1954. Festinger and his colleagues joined the group to find out what would happen when the world didn't come to an end on that date. Many of Keech's followers were so strongly committed to this belief that they had left jobs, given away possessions, left spouses, and so on in preparation for their rescue on a flying saucer at midnight on 20 December. However, no visitor from Clarion arrived to take them to their saucer. There was no great flood before dawn. After 4 am, Keech received a 'message' stating that the 'God of Earth' had decided to spare the planet: 'The little group, sitting all night long, had spread so much light that God had saved the world from destruction'.

Festinger argued that taking steps to avoid dissonance occurs when people have committed themselves to a strong belief, have taken actions that are hard to undo in relation to that belief, and are faced with undeniable disconfirmatory evidence. Some of Keech's disciples were full of joy that their sacrifices had paid off and had saved the world. (Some, however, got rather angry.) Festinger's theory suggests that our actions have a strong influence on our attitudes and beliefs. The fact that Keech's followers had given up so much to join her cult meant that most felt the need to reconceptualize their actions to maintain consistency with their beliefs.

Cognitive dissonance can be a driver of confirmation bias. We all have our personal beliefs, prejudices, and biases, and they often help us make sense of the world and navigate our way through life without falling overboard. Looking for disconfirmation is often counterintuitive and seems almost unnatural, so much so that discovering evidence that goes against what we believe or the actions we have taken can be a very psychologically uncomfortable feeling. As a result, we might reinterpret the world to make it fit with our beliefs thereby avoiding cognitive dissonance. Cognitive dissonance is, therefore, implicated in the motivated rejection of science: when new facts are not consistent with previous actions then we might reinterpret reality to fit in with our prior beliefs.

CONFIRMATION BIAS REVISITED: THE NEUROPSYCHOLOGY OF CONFIRMATION BIAS

In fact, being presented with views that run counter to strongly held beliefs – particularly religious or political beliefs – seems to have the same effect as being faced with a physical threat and some of the evidence for this comes from studies of the brain. According to research by Kaplan, Gimbel, and Harris (2016), there are neural systems that govern resistance to changing one's beliefs. The default mode network in the brain is active when one's mind wanders or is focusing inwards (among other things). It is not normally active when we are engaged in some kind of goal-directed activity or dealing with external reality. The researchers found that the DMN was activated when people were faced with evidence that went against their beliefs. It's as if the brain had put its fingers in its ears and shouted, 'La, la, la!' so it couldn't hear what the external world was saying.

The amygdala is a part of the brain that mediates emotions, especially fear. In another study in the US, Kanai, Feilden, Firth, and Rees (2011) found that conservatives, in particular, have, on average, a thicker amygdala than liberals. Conservatism by definition refers to opposition to change and avoidance of anything that threatens traditional values. It looks as if the brain here has built up a neurophysiological defence mechanism against contradictory ideas.

In addition to the effect caused by pre-existing beliefs and prejudices, Erisen, Lodge, and Taber (2014) discuss 'affective contagion' where the initial feelings that are aroused when (socio-political) information is presented unconsciously colour the subsequent conscious considerations that lead to attitude construction. They conducted experiments to find out what the effect might be of unconscious priming prior to political information processing. Priming can be triggered by contextual cues such as the physical appearance of the candidate, emotive symbols such as the Statue of Liberty in the background of a political candidate's ad, and music, and even the effects of the order of the names on a ballot paper. These create an affective bias that drives motivated reasoning and attitude construction.

THE IRRATIONAL PERSISTENCE OF BELIEF

Given that people can have faulty beliefs and mental models, how do we go about correcting them? The theoretical physicist, Max Planck, was not very optimistic on this point: 'the new scientific truth does not triumph by convincing its opponents and making them see the light, but rather because its opponents eventually die, and a new generation grows up that is familiar with it' (Planck, 1948).

There is a lot of research evidence since the work of Festinger demonstrating that correcting a misperception can be very hard to do. Many researchers use the *belief perseverance paradigm* in which an incorrect statement is made and then subsequently corrected to see what effect the correction has on attitudes or beliefs. There appears to be a 'continued influence effect' of misinformation even after a correction or new evidence is presented (Hamby, Ecker, & Brinberg, 2019). The attempt to avoid cognitive dissonance can lead to a strengthening of beliefs that do not fit the evidence. In cases where mistaken beliefs or misinformation is corrected, there can at times be what is known as *contrary updating* or the *backfire effect*. This occurs when people with a particular belief encounter unwelcome information and, rather than them challenging the new information, their original view comes to be believed even more strongly, which cognitive dissonance theory would predict.

Bail et al. (2018) found that US Democrats and Republicans who were exposed to tweets from liberal and conservative Twitter bots increased political polarization. The researchers recruited US Republican and Democrat voters who used Twitter at least three times a week. They were asked a number of questions about social policy issues using a seven-point scale as well as questions about political attitudes and their use of social media. Some of the Republicans and some of the Democrats were offered $11 to follow a Twitter bot (an automated Twitter account) that would retweet 24 messages each day for a month. The bot that the Republican group was to follow was a 'liberal' Twitter bot and the Democrat group was following a 'conservative' Twitter bot. The bots retweeted messages randomly drawn from a sample of 4,176 political Twitter accounts. There was also a control group of Republicans and of Democrats. They were also paid $ 18 to write weekly surveys of the tweets they received. Using Twitter as an echo chamber where views that you hold are being repeated back to you should tend to reinforce one's views. If you are then exposed to repeated views contrary to the ones that you hear, you might expect people to moderate their views at least a little. In fact, the researchers found that the views that people had become even more entrenched when faced with contrary opinion. In yet another example of the backfire effect, conservatives exposed to liberal Twitter bots tended to exhibit significantly more conservative views; however, liberals showed only a slight non-significant tendency to more liberal attitudes when exposed to conservative Twitter feeds.

Flynn et al. (2017) distinguish between being uninformed and being misinformed. If you are uninformed, then you have not been told or have not read anything about the topic (not that this stops people from arguing). Being misinformed is much more pernicious. To be misinformed means that one has taken on board some kind of 'fake news' leading to misperceptions about some aspect of the world. Examples include the sizeable gap between the actual number of foreign born residents in a country and the misperceptions of what that number is. In 2014, polling data for Hungary and Italy in particular showed that the number of immigrants people thought were in the country was three times greater than the number that were actually there. This misperception probably boosted the support for the right-wing parties that took over in those countries. There are also faulty beliefs about the dangers of vaccines, and about the ability of garlic and hot baths to cure the COVID-19 coronavirus, and so on.

An example of the strong views of relatively uninformed people was found by Kuklinski, Quirk, Jerit, Schweider, and Rich (2000) who conducted a telephone survey of Illinois residents in the US where groups were given either relevant facts about welfare or a multiple-choice quiz about those facts. Along with a control group, they were asked their opinions about two welfare policy issues. While all participants presented highly inaccurate beliefs about welfare, the least informed people were the most confident in their answers. Providing relevant facts had no influence on the opinions they espoused.

Nyhan and Reifler (2010) conducted an experiment where participants read a mock newspaper article in which a political figure made a statement that reinforced a widespread misperception. The articles were about weapons of mass destruction (WMD) in Iraq, the effects of tax cuts, and stem cell research. Some participants were given a correction immediately after the incorrect report and a control group did not receive the correction. The misperception that Iraq had WMD lasted long after the end of the Iraq war in the US. The mock article contained information that WMD had been found in Iraq and the correction immediately after made clear that no WMD had been found. Participants are categorized on a range from very liberal (–3) to very conservative (+3) on a seven-point scale. While liberals tended to disagree that Iraq had WMD more than controls, the conservative group showed a backfire effect where they were more likely to believe that Iraq had WMD than controls. This is also an example of *belief polarization.*

Misperceptions as a result of receiving misinformation are not only due to the misinformation itself but also to the kinds of memory organization and integration that take place when we try to make sense of the world. By so doing, we can generate a coherent account of the information we receive, which may involve filling in any gaps in that information by making inferences. This has consequences when a corrective message is presented pointing out that the original information was incorrect in some way. Chan, Jones, Hall Jamieson, and Albarracin (2017) refer to this process as 'debunking'. They point out that a corrective message needs to be sufficiently detailed to overcome the previously formed model. Simply labelling something as incorrect, without a sufficiently detailed reason why, means that the only coherent model a person has is the one generated from the misinformation in the first place and hence the one that is likely to be remembered.

The results of their meta-analysis showed that if people are able to elaborate on the misinformation and generate arguments in support of it, it is hard thereafter to get them to change their views. So, Chan et al.'s first recommendation is to attempt to reduce arguments that support misinformation (although it is rather vague on how one would do that). Their second recommendation was to 'engage audiences in scrutiny and counterarguing of misinformation'. People should try to be their own fact checkers. Finally, they recommended that new information be introduced as part of the debunking message. This allows the initial faulty mental model to be superseded by a new corrected one.

De keersmaecker and Roets (2017) looked at the effects of cognitive ability on what (Hamby et al., 2019) subsequently labelled the 'continued influence effect' of misinformation. They found that the degree to which people succumb to it depended to a certain extent on cognitive ability. In this case, cognitive ability was based on the results of a ten-item vocabulary test from the Wechsler Adult Intelligence Scale (WAIS). This WAIS subtest involves being presented with a target word and choosing the closest synonym from a list of five other words. There were two groups of participants who were presented with a description of a young woman and asked to evaluate her on a number of dimensions. The control group simply had this task but the experimental group was also given a statement about her having been arrested for stealing drugs and selling them which she had been doing for two years before they were asked to evaluate her. Subsequently, this group were told that the information about the drug selling was false and the description of her was re-presented with the drug stealing section struck through. They were then asked to re-evaluate her with the corrected information. Results showed that participants with higher cognitive ability levels changed their attitude to the woman so that they were similar to those of the control group. Those with lower cognitive ability levels showed a continued influence effect of the original misinformation. Their attitudes did change but to a lesser degree than the higher ability participants.

Misinformation, then, has a tendency to persist, and this persistence seems to be related to personality, political leanings, and cognitive ability. There is a danger of stereotyping based on these results. There are intelligent and open-minded conservatives and closed-minded liberals of low ability.

SUMMARY

Despite familiarity with throwing things, dropping them and so on, people's mental models of simple physical phenomena can be mistaken. Examples of pre-Newtonian physics can be found in science fiction films where, for example, engines seem to be firing as a rocket approaches a space station despite the fact that this means the rocket is accelerating towards it. People can have misapprehensions about natural phenomena such as hurricanes, flooding, greenhouse gas emissions, and the like.

Faulty reasoning can also be the product of 'directionally motivated reasoning' where our goals dictate what information to pay attention to and what to dismiss. When information runs counter to our prior beliefs and prejudices this has an effect in the brain itself triggering either the DMN switching attention away from what we are hearing or even triggering a fear response.

Another effect of new information contradicting one's prior beliefs is cognitive dissonance where one's beliefs seem at odds with one's actions. Avoidance of cognitive dissonance along with confirmation bias can be a driver of much our behaviour. This was investigated in a number of famous studies by Festinger in the 1950s.

Attempts to correct misperceptions or mistaken beliefs can sometimes backfire leading to a strengthening of a mistaken belief rather than a questioning of one's views. Cognitive dissonance seems to be underpinning at least some aspects of the irrational persistence of beliefs.

SUGGESTED FURTHER READING

Cooper, J. (2007). *Cognitive dissonance: 50 years of a classic theory.* London, UK: Sage.

Alcock, J. (2018). *Belief: What it means to believe and why our convictions are so compelling*. Amherst, NY: Prometheus.

Lombrozo, T., & Vasilyeva, N. (2017). Causal explanation. In M. Waldmann (Ed.), *Oxford handbook of causal reasoning* (pp. 415–432). Oxford, UK: Oxford University Press.

9

THE TRUTH, THE WHOLE TRUTH, AND NOTHING LIKE THE TRUTH

INTRODUCTION

I am sitting in front of a laptop typing this. I may be biased or prejudiced or mistaken but I do believe the laptop in front of me is real. However, because of overwhelming and verifiable evidence and the fact that other people can attest that my laptop is real and that I am sitting in front of it, I know for a fact that I am sitting in front of a real laptop. Now, there have been those who have denied that there are such things as facts. Nietzsche argued that there are no facts only interpretations of the world, the virtual reality model our brains generate. Some postmodernist thinkers, mainly in the second half of the 20th century, have claimed that truth or facts are illusions; that science is not, as it claims, objective but is subjective since it is the product of a particular culture and socio-political organization. Rather than dealing with absolutes, it is relative and no different from other equally valid forms of narrative. This creates a bit of a paradox in that the assertions they make about science are presumably illusions as well. They are also the result of a particular culture and socio-political organization.

They might claim that facts are too limiting and that we should rely on opinion rather than 'facts'. For example:

'Reason is whatever the norms of the local culture believe it to be' (Putnam, 1983, p. 235).
'There is no unique truth, no unique objective reality' (Gellner, 1985, p. 84).

To take the first of these two assertions – I have a rule that says: 'If I shoot a high velocity bullet through my head, I will be dead', and then assert: 'I am not dead'. Is there any culture that can possibly conclude that I have just shot myself through the head with a high velocity bullet? That would not be a reasonable conclusion in any culture. As for the second, if there is no unique truth, one might ask questions such as 'How many gravitational constants are there?' 'If I divide velocity (e.g., 80 kilometres per hour) by time (e.g., 2 hours), how many different distances will I have travelled?' However, given that the laptop before me is a shared interpretation as is the fact that I have two sisters, that the 3rd January follows the 2nd January, and so on, I am going to continue to use the word 'fact' to cover these verifiable assertions. As Peter van Inwagen has said: 'If a doctor says I have cancer of the gut, whether that is true depends on what is going on in my gut, and not on what is going on in my doctor's mind' (quoted in O'Callaghan, 2017).

Another argument is that so-called facts can become outdated or shown to be false over time. But are we likely to find in the future that Belgium invaded Germany at the beginning of the second world war? That said, there are those who deny that the holocaust happened, or who deny that there is such a thing as evolution despite the verifiable evidence that they are wrong. If there are people who think that Belgium invaded Germany, maybe they could get away with it these days by claiming that this is an 'alternative fact' of the type found in Philip K. Dick's 'The Man in the High Castle'. Alternatively, they might claim that they are entitled to their opinion. However, in what way can one be entitled to an opinion that is demonstrably false? Entitlement suggests that there is a legitimate basis for such a belief, but in such cases none exists. On the other hand, if a situation is undecided or unclear, then it can be very useful to have opinions (or hypotheses) until the situation is clarified, assuming it can be. However, my aim in this section is not really to get into a philosophical argument about reality or whether we live in a Matrix world, but rather to look at some of the possible psychological reasons why people think that demonstrably false ideas are actually true.

A number of psychiatric illnesses can lead to delusional beliefs at odds with reality. Panic attacks, depression, bipolar disorder, schizophrenia, and so on can seriously affect the way one interprets the world. Such mental disorders or disturbances can lead to emotional reasoning. Two people can therefore, sometimes literally, 'see things differently' depending on their state of mind. However, having a delusional belief that is clearly false is not quite the same thing as having particular *interpretation* of reality. Some personality types can be more prone to unsubstantiated beliefs than others, and some personality disorders can lead to false beliefs. For example, the 5th edition of the Diagnostic and Statistical Manual of Mental Disorders lists nine criteria for diagnosing someone as having Narcissistic Personality Disorder (NPD). Some clinical psychologists would add to or amplify some of those criteria. For example, if evidence is shown to someone with NPD that contradicts their 'grandiose sense of self-importance', they are apt to falsify the evidence and even believe in their own lie because it conflicts with their view of themselves as special. If they are criticized, they will react angrily and hurl abuse at their detractors. These reactions are believed to be due to their underlying low self-esteem. At the same time, another effect of the disorder is to make them driven to succeed, hence many who have NPD can be very successful businessmen or women and become very rich and powerful.

However, we lesser mortals are likely to be subject to more general everyday biases in the way we view the world and hence in what we might regard as true. Nevertheless, I am going to assume that there is a real world out there and that we have evolved to navigate our way around it successfully enough to be able to feed ourselves, procreate, and avoid being eaten.

BELIEF AND DISORDERS OF BELIEF

As we have seen, our mental models of this world may, at times, be faulty. Our culture, personal history, and personality motivate our actions and our reasoning, and influence what we believe to be true. Whenever our beliefs overlap with reality then we can be said to have knowledge about the world rather than just beliefs, opinions or theories. Up until now, I have discussed knowledge in terms of what you have learned about the world. Some of it may be useful, some of it may be wrong. In this section, I am talking about knowledge* (knowledge prime) where your knowledge mirrors reality (see Figure 9.1). You might 'know' that the earth is flat, but you would be wrong. The mental model of the world in this case is faulty.

Being a hypothesis, a belief should be provisional until it gets updated by new information. However, that rarely happens. Stanovich (1993) has argued that there should be an equivalent to dyslexia and dyscalculia relating to people's rationality. He calls it *dysrationalia* and defines it as a disorder of belief formation and consistency, or a difficulty in assessing how to achieve one's goals. It is also unrelated to intelligence which means that clever people can make stupid decisions (Bruine de Bruin, Parker, & Fischhoff, 2007; Robson, 2019; Stanovich & West, 2008; Stanovich, West, & Toplak, 2013). Apart from measures of thinking bias investigated by Stanovich and West, a number of tests have been developed that measure aspects of what one could call dysrationalia. Bruine de Bruin et al. (2007)

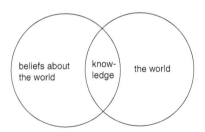

FIGURE 9.1 Beliefs, knowledge and reality (after Plato).

developed a test (an aggregate of seven decision-making tasks) that seemed to show that decision-making competence was mostly independent of cognitive ability. Those who performed better on the test seemed to make better decisions in life leading to fewer negative life events.

Kahan (2017) developed a scale to test the 'ordinary science intelligence' which included measures of general scientific knowledge, scientific methods, quantitative reasoning, and cognitive reflection items designed to show degrees of resistance to cognitive biases. Naturally people varied between relative ignorance to scientifically knowledgeable. However, despite their shared knowledge of science, liberal Democrats in the US and conservative Republicans diverged markedly with the biggest gap between them at the most knowledgeable end of the spectrum. Indeed, the belief polarization between the Democrat wing of US politics and the Republican wing seems to generate irrational decision-making. Al Gore has been trying very hard over the years to explain the dangers of climate change. However, he is a Democrat and stood for the presidency losing to George W. Bush. '[Al Gore] firmly belongs to only one tribe. So by definition, it means the other tribe must reject him—and everything he stands for' (Hayhoe & Schwartz, 2017, p. 67). This is a further example of belief formation being disrupted by an irrelevant aspect (Al Gore is a Democrat) of the issue (climate change) causing otherwise intelligent people to make stupid decisions.

One of Stanovich's examples of dysrationalia was a story of two former teachers who left their employment because their school was teaching about the Holocaust which they were convinced was a myth (Stanovich, 1993). They then sent 6,000 letters to parents and Congress to complain about the teaching of this 'myth'. Another was the fact that Sir Arthur Conan Doyle, a very intelligent man and creator of Sherlock Holmes, was taken in by mediums and believed in fairies. Robson (2019) provides the example of a 68-year-old theoretical particle physicist who found a Czech bikini model on the Matel.com dating site and arranged to meet up in Bolivia. When he arrived, he found that she had had to fly to another photo shoot in Brussels, and she asked him to pick up her suitcase she had left. He was arrested and charged with smuggling cocaine. To an outside observer, a Czech bikini model showing an interest in a 68-year-old physicist would appear suspicious at the very least.

Dysrationalia can apply to solving apparently simple problems such as those in Box 9.1.

The second item in Box 9.1 is an example of *survivorship bias* or survival bias where people focus on the survivors to learn lessons rather than from the ones that failed. The Center for Naval Analyses, despite the title, did not think things through. Survivorship bias can be seen in a range of fields. The ex-voto chapel of Saint Pierre in Notre Dame de la Garde in Marseille is filled with votive offerings (ex-votos) by sailors to the Virgin Mary for rescuing them from

---

BOX 9.1 EXAMPLES TO TEST FOR DYSRATIONALIA

1. *There is a bottle of wine that costs €10. The wine in the bottle costs €9 more than the bottle itself. How much does the bottle cost?*

   The answer that usually comes first to mind is to say €'1' which would be wrong. It is an intuitive answer but not one that has been thought through. People tend to ignore the 'more than' phrase. Consider this alternative:

   There is a bottle of wine that costs €10. The wine in the bottle costs €9 more than the bottle itself. How much does the wine cost?

   This version of the problem forces you to analyze the problem more thoroughly.

2. Abraham Wald was a statistician and member of the USA's Statistical Research Group during the Second World War. The Center for Naval Analyses wanted to ensure that their aircraft could survive the damage caused by bullets so they analyzed the pattern of bullet holes in the returning aircraft with a view to improving the armour there. Abraham Wald realized that the Navy had been analyzing the planes that had returned safely. He, therefore, recommended that the aircraft should be reinforced where there were no dots since damage there meant the aircraft didn't return home (Figure 9.2).

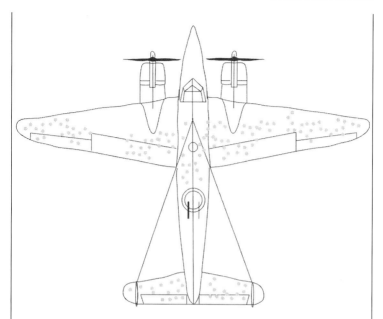

FIGURE 9.2 Aggregate patterns of bullet holes in planes returning from bombing runs. (based on a drawing attributed to McGeddon at https://commons.wikimedia.org/wiki/File:Survivorship-bias.png).

shipwreck and pirates. She is believed to watch over sailors in the Mediterranean. However, those that have been lost to shipwreck or taken by pirates do not leave ex-votos, only the survivors do.

MOTIVATED IGNORANCE, AND REAL IGNORANCE

'There is a cult of ignorance in the United States, and there always has been. The strain of anti-intellectualism has been a constant thread winding its way through our political and cultural life, nurtured by the false notion that democracy means that "my ignorance is just as good as your knowledge"' (Asimov, 1980).

Although Asimov wrote this in the 1980s, many scientists and thinkers today believe that science denialism has got worse. Scientific American has an entire journal devoted to it (2017, volume 317). In the previous chapter, I discussed motivated reasoning. The other side of that coin is *motivated ignorance*:

'Speer recounts an occasion where his trusted friend and colleague, Karl Hanke, after visiting a concentration camp (probably Auschwitz), reportedly advised him never to accept an invitation to inspect one under any circumstances: "I did not query him, I did not query Himmler, I did not query Hitler, I did not speak with personal friends. I did not investigate – for I did not want to know what was happening there"' (Quoted in Lynch, 2016, pp. 505–506).

The study of ignorance is *agnotology* and includes the study of why we are not supposed to know something. That is, it's the study of ignorance as a strategy, often in support of vested interests. An example is that of Lindsey Graham, a Chair of the Senate Committee on the Judiciary in 2019, had stated that it would be 'very disturbing' to find evidence of a *quid pro quo* in President Trump's conversations with the Ukrainian President. Transcripts of the President's phone calls were released during the impeachment inquiry that provided such evidence. However, the senator said that he wouldn't look at it. That way he was able to keep his views intact and avoid cognitive dissonance.

Motivated ignorance covers situations such as avoiding going to see the doctor about the cough you've had for the past six weeks because you don't want to find out that there is something seriously wrong with you. Or it might mean that you suspect your partner is having an affair but don't check up on it in case you find it's true. For the individual, the consequence of motivated ignorance is that they might end up feeling much worse in the end. For governments, the consequence of motivated ignorance might be the deaths of thousands or millions of its citizens. There are many examples where governments do not want to find out if there are problems with a policy and will not countenance criticism. Examples include the Soviet agricultural policy from 1928–1932, the Great Famine in China during the Great Leap

Forward, as well as more general topics such as governments' responses to smoking, sugar, and obesity. There have been occasions where governments and businesses have actively attempted to ensure ignorance about areas such as global warming, acid rain, the ozone hole, the dangers of pesticides, tobacco, and passive smoking (Oreskes & Conway, 2010):

> '[...] in a tragic example of willful blindness, Trump has abolished a rule requiring federal agencies to consider how large federal projects affect climate change and how climate impacts, such as sea level rises and drought, might affect the long-term viability of the projects themselves. This is akin to erecting a building on a fault zone without considering earthquakes'. (Kenneth Kimmell, Guardian, Sunday, 16 April 2017)

Another example of motivated, or possibly real, ignorance is the occasion when Jim Inhofe, Chairman of the Senate's Environment and Public Works Committee, threw a snowball in the Senate to somehow show that there was no such thing as global warming. Yet another example is one of Donald Trump's tweets on 6 December 2013: 'Ice storm rolls from Texas to Tennessee - I'm in Los Angeles and it's freezing. Global warming is a total, and very expensive, hoax!' In response to this kind of thinking, in 2014, the US comedian and political commentator, Stephen Colbert, tweeted: 'Global warming isn't real because I was cold today! Also, great news: World hunger is over because I just ate'. With a bit of effort one can do something about real ignorance. Motivated ignorance, for all the reasons mentioned about confirmation bias and the irrational persistence of beliefs, is more intractable.

CONSPIRATORIAL THINKING

Along with cultural beliefs, dogmas, faith, and so on, vested interests can influence and motivate our thinking, and our beliefs can become invested with an emotional attachment. Views about Holocaust denial or that the universe was created within the last 6,000 years can be strongly held. As we have seen, rejecting a belief can often be harder to do than continuing to accept it and looking for evidence, however flimsy, to back it up. Avoidance of cognitive dissonance, motivated ignorance, and confirmation bias are examples of *motivated cognition*. As a result, we can end up being susceptible to self-deception, wishful thinking, the rejection of science, or to a belief in conspiracy theories.

Bertrand Russell wrote, with a degree of hyperbole, that, 'The opinions that are held with passion are always those for which no good ground exists; indeed, the passion is the measure of the holder's lack of rational conviction. Opinions in politics and religion are almost always held passionately' (Russell, 1928, p. 3). He was referring to that class of opinions where there can be no obvious clear answer or where an idea has not yet been tested. It is perfectly possible to hold opinions with passion for which good grounds do exist. Some opinions may turn out to be true (then we have knowledge* rather than opinion) and others may be shown to be false (although that doesn't always stop people believing them).

If fake news and conspiracy theories get repeated often enough, then people will start to believe them despite mere repetition being an illogical basis for thinking that an assertion is true. From a political strategy website discussing 'tools and tips for winning elections', the main advice is 'repeat, repeat, repeat'. Social media often tend to provide an echo chamber where fake news gets repeated. Thus, more than a quarter of US adults think the government is hiding aliens in Area 51. Just under a quarter think 9/11 was an inside job and that climate change is a hoax (YouGov survey January 2019; Inhofe, 2012). A fabricated story about a pizza restaurant being the centre of a Clinton campaign paedophile ring during the 2016 US presidential election was believed by 17% of Clinton supporters and 46% of Trump supporters. There are many internet blogs inveighing against vaccination and denying the science behind it. This science denial merges into a belief, for example, that climate science is a hoax: a conspiracy, presumably involving many tens of thousands of scientists around the world and millions of dodgy thermometers.

As mentioned in Chapter 7, most people do not prick up their ears and listen carefully when political ads appear on the media. Their attention is peripheral. However, if a phrase or epithet or idea is repeated often enough, then that will eventually be remembered. As a persuasive technique, repetition in an emotional speech, whether the assertions are true or dubious, can be very effective indeed. Martin Luther King Jr's repetition of 'I have a dream' was effective for this reason. Stating something three times in this way seems to have the optimum rhetorical impact. Aesthetics, therefore, can have a strong role to play in techniques of persuasion because, as with the Keats effect, it seems to be easier for us to process the information when the form it takes is pleasing.

In 1977, Hasher, Goldstein, and Toppino (1977) gave participants 60 plausible assertions at 2-week intervals about topics in geography, politics, science, sports, and so on. Some were true, such as, 'lithium is the lightest of all metals', and some were false such as, 'it takes twice as much force to move a ton of freight by railroad as it does by truck'. Participants were asked to estimate their validity on a seven-point scale. A total of 20 of the first 60 statements were repeated in subsequent presentations. What they found was that the repeated statements significantly increased participants' belief in their validity whether they were true of false. This has come to be known as the *illusory truth effect*. Brashier, Eliseev, and Marsh (2020) found that initial fact checking protected people from the illusory truth effect but only if the person had relevant background knowledge to begin with. Furthermore, young people often needed a 'nudge' to check the validity of a statement whereas older people did so spontaneously (Brashier, Umanath, Cabeza, & Marsh, 2017).

WHO IS SUSCEPTIBLE TO FAKE NEWS?

The illusory truth effect is widespread and can be seen in the impact of adverts, political propaganda, social media, etc. Vosoughi, Deb, and Aral (2018) found that falsehoods (fake news) in social media travel faster and get repeated more than political assertions that are factual. Misinformation can thereby get solidified into conspiracy theories depending on the individual's cognitions. It is even possible to predict that a person will believe a particular conspiracy theory if they already believe in another one. Conspiratorial thinking seems to lead to a correlation between beliefs in one conspiracy (such as: NASA faked the moon landing) and can lead people to a rejection of climate science or that HIV causes AIDS or a belief that vaccinations cause autism (Lewandowsky & Oberauer, 2016; Lewandowsky, Oberauer, & Gignac, 2013). For example, Rush Limbaugh, a right-wing American talk show host, has espoused a number of conspiracy theories on CFCs and the ozone layer, Obama's birthplace, blaming Obama for bringing Ebola to the USA, etc. He has since created a new conspiracy theory that coronavirus was the common cold and an anti-Trump conspiracy.

Along with political leaning, there appears to be a further correlation between this kind of thinking and authoritarian attitudes, low empathy, closed-mindedness (not being open to new experiences), and being male (bear in mind these are correlations and not deterministic. Fortunately, being male doesn't automatically make you a flat-earther). These findings can be explained to some extent by a phenomenon known as *social dominance orientation* (SDO). SDO is a psychological preference for hierarchical social structures (Pratto, Sidanius, Stallworth, & Malle, 1994). Thus, people who score highly in SDO espouse ideologies that assume there is an inherent and inevitable inequality among social groups; hence, a belief in capitalism, meritocracy, and a tendency to racism and sexism. It is negatively correlated with empathy, tolerance, and altruism. Low scores suggest a view that resists categorizing people and is more egalitarian. Thus, according to Pratto et al. (1994, p. 741), there are 'two varieties of legitimizing myths: hierarchy-enhancing legitimizing myths, which promote greater degrees of social inequality, and hierarchy-attenuating legitimizing myths, which promote greater social equality'.

People can also be divided in their opinions due to cognitive style. One can make a judgement on a topic such as vaccination based on the degree to which one is willing to engage in analytic thinking. A reduced Actively Open minded Thinking (AOT) would be an example of dysrationalia. Lewandowsky and Oberauer (2016) included a preference for sticking with simplifying heuristics rather than analyzing complex issues as one of the reasons behind the motivated rejection of science along with biased risk assessment and adopting a 'conspiracist ideation'. Hence South African president Thabo Mbeki did not believe that HIV and AIDS are related leading to his refusal to allow drugs to treat the disease regarding them as 'poisons'. Between 343,000 and 365,000 are estimated to have died as a result of his policies and relying on treatments using herbal remedies.

Other researchers have shown that a variety of personality types are more disposed to conspiracy theories and fake news than others. Bronstein, Pennycook, Bear, Rand, and Cannon (2018) recruited over 900 participants through Amazon's Mechanical Turk and presented them with 12 false and 12 real news stories. They also conducted a series of measures using a number of inventories such as the Peters et al. Delusion Inventory (PDI; Peters, Joseph, Day, & Garety, 2004); cognitive style measured via the AOT scale (Stanovich & West, 2007); the Cognitive Reflection Test (Frederick, 2005); the DOG scale measuring dogmatism (Altemeyer, 2002); and the Religious Fundamentalism Scale (Altemeyer & Hunsberger, 1992). As for their findings, the title of their paper sums them up quite neatly: 'Belief in Fake News is Associated with Delusionality, Dogmatism, Religious Fundamentalism, and Reduced Analytic Thinking'.

Much of the research on the motivated rejection of science has been conducted in the US due to the cultural divide between liberals and conservatives (Democrats and Republicans) that has already been discussed. For example, strong supporters of free-market economics are most likely to reject the science of climate change (Cook & Lewandowsky, 2016; Kahan, Braman, Slovic, Gastil, & Cohen, 2009). Kahan et al. asked people for their views on nanotechnology, a topic that did not divide opinion amongst the respondents due to its relative unfamiliarity. However, when they presented information about the risks and benefits of nanotechnology, liberals and conservatives were divided along their worldview with liberals being more risk averse and conservatives focussing on the economic benefits.

As we have seen, overcoming conspiracy theories or the motivated rejection of science is far from easy. Schmid and Betsch (2019) ran a number of experiments to find out what kind of strategy might mitigate the influence of science denial. They found that providing facts along with identifying and using the rhetorical techniques science denialists use can be effective. Finding ways to combat conspiracy theories and science rejection is of immense importance. Anti-vaxxers are beginning to cause epidemics of diseases we had thought almost eradicated. Denying climate science has a qualitatively different effect since climate change is likely to have a destructive impact on human civilization as well as causing mass extinctions unless it is taken seriously and dealt with urgently. With evidence of dysrationality, motivated ignorance, and the avoidance of cognitive dissonance rife among some very important and influential groups, Walter Quattrociocchi has suggested, echoing Asimov some 37 years later, that 'the age we live in should be renamed from the Information Age to the Age of Credulity' (Quattrociocchi, 2017, p. 63).

SUMMARY

There have been philosophical arguments about the nature of truth and what 'facts' are. However, assuming there is a verifiable state of affairs in the world, we can compare our beliefs and opinions to what we discover about the world to see how far they overlap. There are many reasons why someone may have beliefs about the world that do not correspond with reality. Some of these come under the general rubric of motivated cognition. When there is a disorder of belief formation and consistency, or a difficulty in assessing how to achieve one's goals then there is evidence of dysrationalia.

An example of dysrationalia and motivated cognition is motivated ignorance where one deliberately avoids finding something out in case it conflicts with prior beliefs and prejudices. This can be ultimately damaging to an individual or to a society when a government is guilty of ignoring information ('shooting the messenger').

By dint of repetition along with motivated reasoning, fake news can lead to conspiracy theories. Repetition is enough to allow an assertion to be believed even after information that the assertion was false. Mud sticks.

Belief in one conspiracy theory is predictive of belief in others and belief in conspiracies and fake news is correlated with political (generally conservative) ideology, dogmatism, and reduced analytic thinking. The consequences of some aspects of motivated cognition can be extremely serious.

SUGGESTED FURTHER READING

Lewandowsky, S., Oberauer, K., & Gignac, G. E. (2013). Nasa faked the moon landing—therefore, (climate) science is a hoax: An anatomy of the motivated rejection of science [Article]. *Psychological Science, 24*(5), 622–633. Retrieved from https://doi.org/10.1177/0956797612457686.

Oreskes, N., & Conway, E. M. (2010). *Merchants of doubt: How a handful of scientists obscured the truth on issues from tobacco smoke to global warming.* New York, NY: Bloomsbury Press.

Prooijen, J.-W. (2018). *The psychology of conspiracy theories.* London, UK: Routledge.

Scientific American (2017). *Return to reason: The science of thought. Scientific American, 317(4).* September 2017. New York, NY: SCIENTIFIC AMERICAN, a Division of Springer Nature America, Inc.

10

MAGICAL THINKING

WHAT IS MAGICAL THINKING?

Magical thinking is the belief that our thoughts or desires alone can cause something to happen or that an event such as a birthdate or the position of some planets can cause you to meet a tall, dark, handsome stranger despite there being no physical causal link between them. Allied to this is the human desire for explanations for phenomena (Keil, 2006; Lombrozo & Vasilyeva, 2017). We can get anxious if we don't have them. In the past, people stuck on a train that stops in the middle of nowhere for no obvious reason got agitated because they didn't know what was happening. When drivers started to tell passengers why the train had stopped, there were fewer complaints. In some cases, it doesn't matter what the explanation is as long as there is one. If there's thunder and you don't know what causes it, then postulating an angry god provides an explanation, and, in a particular culture, a believable one. The ignorance is removed. We don't, therefore, need to expend the effort needed to find out what's really going on when lightning strikes. The culturally accepted, intuitive response suffices.

Superstition, beliefs in the supernatural and religious beliefs are a combination of trying to find an explanation for what would otherwise be inexplicable, an attempt to predict the world, and a mechanism of social cohesion. Some forms of superstitious or magical thinking take the form of what we call 'luck'. A belief in luck is often a combination of associative learning and confirmation bias. If you have a lucky rabbit's foot and you just escape a nasty road accident, then it's just as well you have a lucky rabbit's foot since it caused the car to miss you. It's hard to imagine what the world would be like if lucky objects really were lucky. Think how many hundreds of thousands of lottery millionaires there would be now, how few accidents there would be, how many hundreds of thousands of children do better in exams than expected, and so on. These objects are deemed lucky because the owners have noticed the good luck they bring and ignored all the times when they have brought no such luck. Our knowledge of the world includes the inductive associations we make between one thing (X) and another (Y) such that X seems to cause, or be reliably followed by, Y. Hence, the intuitive, ill-thought-through view that the rabbit's paw must exert a power over the world. It's often a very useful way to make sense of the world, so there is method in your madness. It's just not a very good method.

Associative thinking can be immediate such as when an event (X) is immediately associated with another event (Y). If you flick a switch and a light comes on, you know that the flicking the switch caused the light to come on. If, when you flick the switch, there is a simultaneous bang in the street, it can temporarily be difficult to shake off the belief that switching the light on had caused the bang. Such dubious cause and effect associations can give rise to superstitious thinking particularly in stressful, competitive, or dangerous situations. In the theatre, there are a number of general superstitions. Whistling backstage is assumed to bring bad luck, as is saying 'good luck'. 'Break a leg' is usually said instead. Don't refer to 'Macbeth' in a theatre but rather: 'the Scottish play'. Tennis stars provide a good example of idiosyncratic superstitions. When Serena Williams was on a winning streak, she reportedly did not change her socks as if the socks were the cause of the winning streak. Roger Federer believed that having eight things (racquets and bottles of water) or doing something such as wiping his face eight times contributed to his success. Early in Andy Murray's career, he wore a 'lucky' grey Fred Perry shirt and it was noted that he hadn't stopped winning since he started to wear it, defeating Rafael Nadal and reaching the final of the US Open at the age of 21. The tennis stars seem to have identified a pattern in their behaviour and sought to maintain it. Beck and Forstmeier (2007) argue that, since detecting patterns is an evolved characteristic, superstition is a by-product.

While such personal superstitions may seem irrational to the outside observer, it would be useful to know if they perform any useful function. A study by Damisch, Stoberock, and Mussweiler (2010) suggests that such superstitions can lead to performance improvements in a wide range of areas such as golf, motor dexterity, memory, and anagrams. They conclude that such performance improvements are due to a feeling of increased self-efficacy and confidence. Magical thinking, including superstitions and personal idiosyncratic rituals, seems to be related to a desire for this kind of predictability (Brashier, Umanath, Cabeza, & Marsh, 2017; Keinan, 1994, 2002). They both derive from a desire to impose a reassuring pattern on the world that, in turn, leads to rituals that seem to be useful at reducing stress. That said, there is some evidence that magical explanations for events tend to fade away with age (Brashier et al., 2017), probably due to a greater experience of the world. Sometimes, though, a superstition can co-exist alongside a rational explanation of events: 'God puts you in the path of an HIV-positive lover, but biology causes you to contract the virus from his semen' (Susan Gelman, quoted in Hutson, 2008).

MAGICAL CONTAGION AND SEEING PATTERNS THAT AREN'T THERE

Teigen and Jensen (2011) distinguish between two forms of luck: blind luck (random chance) and magic luck. Blind luck occurs if you survive a tsunami by being in the right place at the right time. Magic luck means that lucky events are due to hidden forces or fate. Believing in luck implies that events are not due to chance but due to some supernatural influence (Darke & Freedman, 1997). Luck, good or bad, can be passed on through a process called *magical contagion*. This refers to the belief that, if two objects or people come into contact, then there can be a magical link between them. Owning a guitar from famous rock star, or a dress worn by Marylin Munroe confers something of the previous owner to the new one. Otherwise, why would you do that when cheaper guitars and dresses abound? At the same time, one might feel uncomfortable wearing a swastika arm band previously worn by Heinrich Himmler (unless one is a neo-Nazi).

Another influence that can give rise to magical thinking is our ability to see patterns in the world even if they are not really there. A pattern of three or four dots can be enough to allow us to see a face. Seeing faces where none exists is known as *pareidolia*. Thus, people have seen faces on Mars, the Virgin Mary in window glass, Jesus' face in an oil slick, and so on. While seeing patterns can lead to superstitious behaviour in humans, the same phenomenon has been found in pigeons. Skinner (1948) found that pigeons used for conditioning experiments that had been kept in cages developed superstitious behaviour. They were fed through a mechanism attached to the cages for a few minutes each day. When the birds had been left without food for a while, Skinner found that the birds repeated the behaviour that they were doing when the food eventually arrived, such as turning counterclockwise or bobbing their head up and down. They subsequently repeated these behaviours in the (pigeon version of) hope that food would, therefore, arrive. One could also view the pigeons' behaviour patterns as equivalent to rituals that they perform to magically produce food.

MAGICAL THINKING AND COGNITIVE STYLE

Superstitious and supernatural beliefs, and religious thinking are universal aspects of human cognition (Boyer, 2008; Gray & Gallo, 2016). Gray and Gallo quote a Gallup poll (Gallup, 2005) showing a high level of belief in the US in psychic phenomena:

42% believe in extrasensory perception (ESP), 31% in telepathy, and 26% in clairvoyance. While sceptics outperformed believers in analytical tasks in Grey and Gallo's studies, they also found that psychic belief was associated with greater life satisfaction; thus, while there are benefits to being a sceptic, there appear to be downsides too.

While supernatural beliefs may be universal, there are individual differences in people's susceptibility to such beliefs. For example, there is a negative correlation between superstitious beliefs and a rational cognitive style (Brankovic, 2019). There is also a positive correlation between superstitious beliefs and a belief in ESP. Swami, Pietschnig, Stieger, and Voracek (2011) also found a correlation between ESP and a range of paranormal beliefs but frequent negative correlations with education level. Even atheists have been shown to exhibit beliefs in a range of supernatural phenomena, although fewer than believers in a deity. The nature of some of these varies from culture to culture. Bullivant, Farias, Lanman, and Lee (2019) studied the beliefs of populations in Brazil, China, Denmark, Japan, UK, and USA. For example, the stand-out supernatural belief among Chinese atheists and agnostics is astrology. Overall, about 18–28% of atheists and between 20% and 38% of agnostics believe that 'significant events are meant to be'. The percentages for both groups are nevertheless considerably lower than for the populations as a whole.

ORIGINS OF MAGICAL THINKING

There are aspects of children's thinking that survive to affect that of adults. We saw in Chapter 2 that babies and young children have an animistic view of the world and are predisposed to assume some form of agency in order to make things happen, from cars moving to the wind blowing. There are many events and phenomena that we cannot, or couldn't in the past, necessarily explain. As a result, we would invent causal explanations that involve some unseen agency such as water spirits, wind gods, dryads, and so on. The belief in invisible external agencies can be bolstered by theory of mind. While this evolved to help us interact in social groups, it can be extended to those external agencies watching over you (gods, saints, spirits).

In trying to make sense of their experience, young children may categorize things based on their superficial features. For example, Gentner and Toupin (1986) presented children with stories that they had to act out by playing characters in the stories. At the end of the stories, in some cases, there was a sentence providing a conclusion in the form of a moral. An example of an original story involved a chipmunk who helped a moose to escape from a frog. The children had to act out a version involving different characters. In one, the characters were obviously semantically related (the chipmunk became a squirrel, the moose became an elk, and the frog became a toad). This was the 'high transparency' condition where the features of the story were clearly related and easily mapped. There was also a 'low transparency' condition where the roles were partly reversed: the elk now played the role of the chipmunk, the toad played the role of the moose, and the squirrel played the frog. A third 'medium transparency' condition had characters that were not semantically related to the originals. Younger children imitated the sequence of actions taken by semantically similar characters in the earlier story but in the medium and low conditions, they tended to produce a 'non-systematic' conclusion. Only when the children understood the underlying systematic rationale for the story were they able to adapt the characters' roles to fit the story's structure.

Similarities in surface features can also lead adults to ignore or be unaware of the underlying structure of a situation. Fraser's (1922/2002) book 'The Golden Bough' provides many examples of superficial similarity used in ritual and magic. For example, to persuade the sky to rain, a shaman may sprinkle water on the parched ground to give the sky a clue as to what is needed. He referred to this kind of thinking as homeopathic magic. For many centuries, educated people used superficial similarity as a basis for analogizing to explain phenomena in the world around them. Colour, for example, was an important feature that allowed associations to be made between an object and something else of the same colour. Different coloured metals were associated with the colours of heavenly bodies, gold and yellow for the sun, silver and white for the moon, iron and red for Mars, copper and green for Venus, and so on. Basing reasoning on superficial features is a kind of magical thinking as it ignores a causal structure (Gentner & Colhoun, 2010; Gentner & Jee, 2010; Gentner & Jeziorski, 1989, 1993). Gentner and Jeziorski discuss the move from alchemy to chemistry and pointed out that the alchemists had a great enthusiasm for analogies. Many of them were derived from ancient Egyptian and Greek theories of the elements (fire, water, earth, and air) that, in turn, combined two each of the qualities: hot, cold, wet, and dry. For example, mercury was regarded as fiery, active, and male; sulphur was watery, passive, and female. Combining them produced a 'marriage'. Gentner and Jeziorski quote Umberto Eco (1990) on Renaissance *hermetism* (a spiritual, philosophical, and magical tradition whose name is taken from the Graeco-Egyptian God Hermês Trismegistos): 'The basic principle is not only that the similar can be known through the similar but also that from similarity to similarity everything can be connected with everything else' (Gentner and Jeziorski, 1993, p. 468).

Explanations and correspondences based on superficial features ignore the underlying causal structure required to explain natural phenomena. If red plants can be used to treat problems of the blood, by what mechanism does the colour manage that? Despite the fact that chemistry and physics took over from alchemy a long time ago, a reliance on homeopathic magic continues. Homeopathic medicine is based on the idea that 'like cures like' despite there being no reason why it should any more than assuming yellow plants have a causal relationship with jaundice or that sprinkling water on the ground will make it rain.

MAGICAL THINKING AS DESIRE FULFILMENT

Aspects of Freud's psychology can be related to magical thinking. Freud (1954) distinguished between what he called *primary process thinking* and s*econdary process thinking.* Primary process thinking is governed by a tension created by the instinctive desires of the *id* (a primitive instinctual component of personality) that seeks immediate gratification through the action of the *pleasure principle.* This principle is an embodiment of our desire to seek pleasure and avoid pain. If a need cannot be immediately fulfilled, because reality gets in the way, there is a tension that the primary process can relieve by creating a mental image of the desire or need through fantasizing, daydreaming or even hallucinating.

Another component of personality is the *ego* which is constrained by the need to deal with the real world where immediate gratification is not always possible. Again, there is a tension which is met by secondary process thinking that actively tries to find something that will satisfy the id's needs and desires. It's the process that directs us to look for a cafe or restaurant when we are hungry and when we are not required to do something else such as go to work. Now, since the id seeks fulfilment of instinctive desires without bothering about constraints in the real world, the mental image created by primary process thinking that encapsulates one's desires and wishes can extend to the belief that those mental images can actually act on the real world. This is a form of magic that leads one to assume that there is a kind of causal link between thoughts (for example, in the form of prayer), symbols and ideas, and the outside world such that those thoughts, symbols, and ideas can influence events in the world. Sticking a pin in a doll representing an enemy should, by this logic, cause the enemy to suffer or die. Freud's primary process thinking is best understood as a useful metaphor to show that one's mental representation of a thing or event can potentially give rise to magical thinking.

PARASKEVITRISKAIDEKAPHOBIA

Paraskevitriskaidekaphobia is fear of Friday the 13th. The number 13 is deemed to be unlucky in many cultures and people often assume or expect bad things to happen then. The fear is strengthened by confirmation bias. If bad things happen on Friday the 13th, then the date is noticed and the assumption made that the date itself somehow caused the bad thing to happen. If bad things happen on Tuesday the 25th, then that's just random luck. The date is not noticed because it is not a culturally recognized bad luck day.

Horoscopes, predictions, and so on work because they rely on confirmation bias and peripheral thinking processes rather than analytical ones. Astrology relies on the fact that very few people either ask or try to work out how the position of a planet can possibly influence your personality or your future. If it's supposed to be something to do with gravitational influences at the time of your birth, then a delivery van outside your window at the time will have more influence than Mercury. Meanwhile, scientists relying on analytical processes have conducted research on the effects of being born at particular times of the year on people's health and personality. Figure 10.1 presents a diagram of the effects of the time of year in which people are born and sums up some of the various effects birth months have been found to have, some of which can have a direct impact on thinking. Bear in mind that most of these are tiny variations from the background population and should not be construed as destiny.

It is perhaps not surprising that there are seasonal differences in health outcomes. There are seasonal variations in infections, in the weather, and in people's diets. Vitamin D levels are affected by dark winter months when we are all wrapped up, and people born in winter tend to be affected by things like winter depression, eczema, and wheezing. Another difference that may affect personality is the amount of light available caused by changes in the day/night cycle. There is some evidence to suggest that this cycle can affect brains as they develop (Logan & McClung, 2019). What is harder to understand is why there seems to be a significantly larger number of celebrities from different walks of life born under Aquarius. But then again, there is a reasonably high probability that you will find random clusters like this by chance.

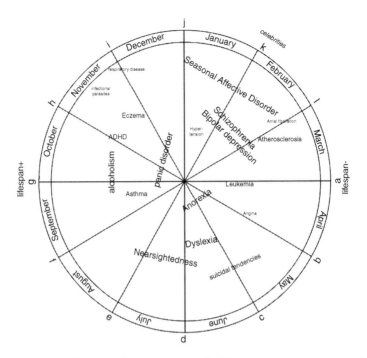

FIGURE 10.1 Some health outcomes and effects on personality depending on birth month and season. (From various sources). The lifespan of those born in the second half of the year appears to be longer than in the first half. ***Leo:*** *If you are a Leo born in August, count yourself lucky.*

THE 'JUST WORLD' HYPOTHESIS

'It's not fair!' is a cry that often comes from the lips of children and finds expression in adult thinking. We have courts that try to mete out justice in the real world, but many people expect that the universe itself will somehow impose justice so that the bad will eventually be punished and the good rewarded – possibly after death. Human social evolution has instilled in (most of) us a sense of fairness. We do not like to see evil rewarded and goodness ignored. We have established complex social institutions to punish the bad and reward the good. However, it is not always the case that the meek inherit the earth. There is a fallacy known as the *just world hypothesis* that refers to a belief that events are not random and that there is a force at work in the universe that administers reward and punishment so that the scales of justice remain in balance. Thus, someone seen to be suffering supposedly deserves it. If someone wins the lottery, they must presumably deserve it.

Lerner and Simmons (1966) wanted to find out under what conditions a person who is seen to be suffering either elicits compassion or is deemed to deserve what is happening to them. In their experiment, participants found themselves witnessing someone taking part in a 'different' experiment receiving painful electric shocks. After ten minutes of this, the participants in one condition were asked to rate the attractiveness of the person receiving the shocks. They were also told that there would be another ten minutes of shocks to be administered. Lerner and Simmons hypothesized that the participants would devalue the victim's personal characteristics given that they were about to watch him suffer yet more, because the idea that an innocent person was about to suffer goes against the view that the world is just. In other conditions, the participants were told that the ten minute bout of pain was at an end, or that the victim would be rewarded in some way, and one in which the participants had some perceived control over the fate of the victim after the first ten-minute session. This last condition produced the most positive view of the victim (the participants showed most compassion). When the suffering could not be stopped, the participants showed the greatest 'rejection' and 'devaluing' of the victim (in Lerner and Simmons' (1966, p. 209) words). In conclusion, they argue that their results provide 'strong support for the assertion that people have a great need to believe in a good and just world'.

An unfortunate effect of the just world fallacy, therefore, is victim blaming. A woman who is raped after a night out having drunk too much 'got what she deserved'. The just world fallacy here manifests itself as a 'reasonable' explanation for suffering. This kind of thinking allows us to believe that the world is predictable and where good things only happen to good people and bad things to bad people. It provides a sense of control and an explanation for otherwise random disasters.

THINGS HAPPEN FOR A REASON

The idea that the universe is just implies that things happen for a reason – in this case, to reward or punish. We are not talking about natural cause and effect here but something supernatural. For example, Jonathan Cahn, a Messianic Jewish pastor, claimed that Hurricane Joaquin that devastated Hawaii in 2015 was a 'sign of God's wrath' because of the legalization of gay marriage, abortion, and the relationship between the UN and Israel (Baggs, 2016). Similarly, Pastor Hank Kunneman of One Voice Ministries stated in 2020 that the US would be protected from coronavirus as Donald Trump is against abortion. It wasn't. Others have also blamed floods in the US and in India on God's displeasure: they are a punishment for moral decay, homosexuality, abortion, same-sex marriage, LGBT + , and so on. In such cases, an event is deemed to be serving some purpose, the alternative being that the universe is random, and many people do not like that idea. Furthermore, if something appears to serve a particular purpose, then some would argue that this shows evidence of design. This is known as the *teleological fallacy*. Yet again, this may be a continuation of a child's view of the world where agency is ascribed to items that seem to do things such as computers and the wind. Keleman (2004) refers to children's 'promiscuous teleology' where they assume that biological entities, such as a lion, have a purpose but so do non-biological entities such as clouds whose purpose is to make it rain. She suggests children may be 'intuitive theists' predisposed to see some kind of design or intention behind natural phenomena.

'LIFE' AFTER DEATH

Of course, the idea that the universe is fair and that people will get their just deserts is one basis for beliefs in life after death. Tobacyk (1983) found that a belief in the paranormal played a role in reducing the fear and threat of death. Indeed, one function of religion is to manage the awareness of death (Norenzayan & Hansen, 2006; Vail, Arndt, & Abdollahi, 2012). It is difficult, in fact paradoxical, to actually imagine one's consciousness no longer existing after death because we are trying to imagine the loss of the ability to imagine. It is, therefore, a short step to believing that one's consciousness will continue to exist after death. Religions offer a narrative whereby you will, indeed, continue to exist in some form. Norenzayan and Hansen (2006) conducted a series of studies during which participants were reminded of death. Among religious participants, this led to an increased expression of religiosity and faith in god(s) or some higher power. It had no effect on non-believers, however.

RELIGIOUS THINKING

Another function of religion is the *worldview defence hypothesis* where cultural beliefs act as a guide to religious behaviour and practices. A person's culture will also determine or influence religious beliefs about the nature of the afterlife, supernatural beings, and events such as miracles. Pennycook, Cheyne, Seli, Koehler, and Fugelsang (2012) proposed an asymmetry between belief and unbelief. Understanding something implies some belief in it, however, provisional. Ideally, this is followed by some form of evaluation to check its believability or to 'unbelieve' it. They argue that a culturally learned spontaneous or intuitive response to something, essentially a heuristic, is the default and that it is initially considered as correct. Only after further effortful analysis, if you are so motivated, can this response be checked for accuracy. Suppose someone says that the recent floods are God's punishment for gay marriage. The first intuitive response, if you believe in a particular type of God, might be, 'Yes, that sounds reasonable.' However, after some deeper reflection, a further response might be, 'So, why did the children have to die?'

Pennycook et al. wanted to find out the effects of certain cognitive styles on magical thinking and belief in supernatural beings. They analyzed a range of demographic variables in their participants: age, sex, degree of religious belief, degree of religious observance, conservatism, cognitive ability, and the one they were particularly interested in, analytic cognitive style. Analytic style was measured using two problems that were versions of the bottle of wine problem (a bat and ball costs $10.10. The bat costs $10 more than the ball. How much is the ball?), and an analogue of Kahneman and Tversky 'lawyers and engineers' problem involving nurses and doctors. An analytic cognitive style is similar to Stanovich's AOT and both involve of Type 2 thinking, whereas the initial intuitive acceptance of an explanation is mediated by Type 1. Their main finding was that an analytic cognitive style, where an initial intuitive response is rejected, was associated with a lack of belief in God and religious concepts such as angels, demons, and hell as well as a lack of belief in other supernatural phenomena such as astrology, ghosts, witchcraft, and so on. In general, conservatives tended to score lower on the active cognitive style which was correlated with some forms of magical thinking.

THE COSTS OF MAGICAL THINKING

Religious practices pose a problem to rational thinking since they involve counterintuitive beliefs, irrational rituals, and often huge costs in the form of severe or cruel sacrifices. Atran and Henrich (2010) argues that the evolution of the cognitive system including the development of prosocial behaviour has predisposed us to believe in supernatural entities and to engage in apparently pointless rituals particularly in large and complex societies.

Religious practices can be seen as the result of cognitive mechanisms such as heuristics (e.g., 'emulation of successful and prestigious individuals'). If people are prepared to martyr themselves for a belief, then there must be something to it as the cost for them is so great. Social and cultural pressures that we have evolved to adhere to also give rise to ritualistic behaviours and costly endeavours such as building stone henges, monumental face sculptures, temples, pyramids, and cathedrals. They suggest that ritualistic activities enhance prosocial behaviour in complex societies and propose 'an approach to devotions (fasting, celibacy, etc.) and rituals as having evolved culturally (at least in part) to deepen people's commitments to counter-intuitive beliefs' (Atran & Henrich, 2010, p. 22).

While religious beliefs and expression vary from religion to religion, all 'hijack' the same cognitive resources (Boyer, 2001, 2008). They constitute a side-effect – an emergent property – of evolved cognitive capacities. As a result, 'Some form of religious thinking seems to be the path of least resistance for our cognitive systems. By contrast, disbelief is generally the result of deliberate, effortful work against our natural cognitive dispositions – hardly the easiest ideology to propagate' (Boyer, 2008, p. 1039).

SUMMARY

Magical thinking is universal and refers to the belief that thoughts, desires, and rituals can cause something to happen. It, therefore, encompasses the view that events can happen without a physical cause. This can be seen in superstitious behaviour. It can also be induced by detecting patterns that do not really exist, as in conspiratorial thinking. Superstitious behaviour can be reinforced by confirmation bias.

Some of its origins can be found in children's thinking such as a reliance on superficial aspects of the world, thus alchemists relied on superficial features of things to try to understand how nature worked. Children also expect the world to be fair and this leads to the just world fallacy and the teleological fallacy, the belief that everything happens for a reason. A potential side-effect of expecting the world to be just is victim blaming – if something bad happens to someone, then they must somehow have deserved it.

Religious thinking involves counterintuitive beliefs and irrational rituals. Cultural beliefs influence religious thinking and behaviour; hence, one function of religion is to defend a culture's worldview. There can often be a cost involved in religious thinking in terms of sacrifices, fasting, monument building, and so on.

SUGGESTED FURTHER READING

Hood, R. W. J., Hill, P. C., & Spilka, B. (2018). *The psychology of religion: An empirical approach* (5 ed.). New York, NY: The Guilford Press.

Hutson, M. (2008, March/April). Magical thinking [Article]. *Psychology Today*, *41*(2), 88–95.

AFTERWORD

Although this book was not originally conceived as being about the role of dual-processing in cognition, it seems, however, to have emerged unbidden from the discussions of the various types of thinking in these chapters. There have been different labels attached to the kinds of thinking we engage in. William James in the 19th century distinguished between 'associative' or 'empirical' and 'true' reasoning with the latter involving more careful analysis. In terms of the evolution of thinking, Toates (2006) has referred to stimulus-based processing and higher-order processing, one being unconscious and automatic and the other under conscious control. Petty and Cacioppo (198) referred to peripheral and central processing routes. Various authors have referred to differences between fast, automatic, associative, evolutionarily old, intuitive, implicit, empirical, heuristic, processes, and slow, controlled, serial, evolutionarily recent, explicit, rational, analytical, ones. Evans (2008) and Evans and Stanovich (2013) have listed a number of attributes of Type 1 and Type 2 processes. While each type has a range of attributes associated with it, they do have a kind of family resemblance with each belonging to a different family. Altogether they present the wide variety of ways of thinking we all engage in.

Animals rely on heuristic responses most of which are innate. I once raised up the corners of a jacket I was wearing and my cat cowered and ran – an innate heuristic response despite never having seen a predatory bird in its life. For humans, biologically primary thinking is easier than biologically secondary, hence our thinking is often influenced by 'folk wisdom' of various kinds ('folk' physics, biology, psychology, economics). Some of the kinds of problems we need to solve are straightforward and can rely on either well-rehearsed procedures or heuristic responses with relatively little demand on WM. Others are difficult and rely on complex mental representations and planning that use up the limited capacity of our WM resources. The same is true of reasoning where can make accurate assessments in familiar contexts but find difficulty when dealing with unfamiliar or abstract situations.

The fact that our rationality is bounded gives rise to a reliance on heuristic processing and hence what have been regarded as 'biases', the major ones being satisficing, confirmation of our views, availability, and over-generalization (representativeness) based on the information we encounter which, unfortunately, can at times lead to racism and collective blame. Indeed, Wikipedia provides a very long list of cognitive biases (https://en.wikipedia.org/wiki/List_of_cognitive_biases). We learn about the world from the data available to us, and if the data are biased then our thinking is in danger of becoming so. The evolution of our cognitive system has also primed us to categorize objects, events and people with the consequent risk of bias. It has led us to succumb to superstition and to engage in religious thinking. Type 2 thinking can override those types of thinking, but, again, with the risk that we ignore our intuitions that may well be appropriate to the circumstance. While we have limitations in our cognitive system such as the limited knowledge we have in our LTM and the limits to our capacity to process information in WM, there are also limitations imposed by the environment in that the information available to us is 'local' and hence different for each individual. Thus, there are individual differences in both our ability to analyze situations and in our desire to do so. Nevertheless, Hinton (2017b) points out that implicit associations we learn are due to the associations of the culture we inhabit, whether we are 'actively open minded' thinkers or not. For example, most Americans' attitude to health care and gun ownership on average is rather baffling to most Europeans whose attitude to those topics is generally quite different.

A drawback of the various studies reported here is that much is based on American culture. In psychology, experiments tend to compare one group with another. The US provides an example of belief polarization between what are referred to as 'liberals' and 'conservatives', a schism that is not quite so wide in, say, most European countries although it certainly exists. Another drawback is the preponderance of studies that tend to show where human thinking goes wrong despite Gerd Gigerenzer and others trying to redress the balance. It should be borne in mind that, if heuristics and biases were detrimental to our well-being, they would have been selected out of our behavioural repertoire. At the same time, it can be difficult to balance the positives and negatives that result from different aspects of human thinking. A person can show intelligence and rationality by analyzing data, reaching objectively accurate conclusions, and making predictions. That same person may also show irrational biases or intolerance of other people's views. People vary and so do the styles and types of thinking they employ in the environment they find themselves in.

The world presents us with a lot to think about and many different ways to think about them, but, at an abstract level, thinking is the mental manipulation of information derived from instinctive responses, learned associations and the immediate environment. The purpose of thinking is to generate representations of the world, real or imaginary, modified by the quality and motivations of the cognitive system doing the thinking in the interests of its survival, and, despite some of the irrational pressures that can get in the way, we have been very successful, so far.

REFERENCES

Alicke, M. D., Klotz, M. L., Breitenbecher, D. L., Yurak, T. J., & Vredenburg, D. S. (1995). Personal contact, individuation, and the better-than-average effect. *Journal of Personality and Social Psychology*, *68*(5), 804–825. Retrieved from https://doi.org/10.1037/0022-3514.68.5.804

Altemeyer, B. (2002). Dogmatic behavior among students: Testing a new measure of dogmatism [Article]. *Journal of Social Psychology*, *142*(6), 713–721. https://doi.org/10.1080/00224540209603931

Altemeyer, B., & Hunsberger, B. (1992). Authoritarianism, religious fundamentalism, quest, and prejudice [Article]. *International Journal for the Psychology of Religion*, *2*(2), 113. Retrieved from https://doi.org/10.1207/s15327582ijpr0202_5

Amabile, T. M. (1996). *Creativity in context*. Boulder, CO: Westview.

Anderson, J. R. (1993). *Rules of the mind*. Hillsdale, NJ: Erlbaum.

Anderson, J. R., & Lebiere, C. (1998). *The atomic components of thought*. Hillsdale, NJ: Lawrence Erlbaum.

Asimov, I. (1980, January 21). *A cult of ignorance. Newsweek*, p. 19.

Atran, S., & Henrich, J. (2010). The evolution of religion: How cognitive by-products, adaptive learning heuristics, ritual displays, and group competition generate deep commitments to prosocial religions. *Biological Theory*, *5*(1), 18–30.

Baggs, M. (2016). *US pastor, who believes floods are God's punishment, flees flooded home*. BBC. Retrieved from http://www.bbc.co.uk/newsbeat/

article/37116661/us-pastor-who-believes-floods-are-gods-punishment-flees-flooded-home

Bail, C. A., Argyle, L. P., Brown, T. W., Bumpus, J. P., Chen, H., Hunzaker, M. B. F., Lee, J., Mann, M., Merhout, F., & Volfovsky, A. (2018, September 11). Exposure to opposing views on social media can increase political polarization. *Proceedings of the National Academy of Sciences of the United States of America, 115*(37), 9216–9221. Retrieved from https://doi.org/10.1073/pnas.1804840115

Baillargeon, R. (1995). A model of physical reasoning in infancy. In C. Rovee-Collier & L. P. Lipsitt (Eds.), *Advances in infancy research* (Vol. 9, pp. 305–371). Ablex.

Ballew, C. C., & Todorov, A. (2007). Predicting political elections from rapid and unreflective face judgments. *Proceedings of the National Academy of Sciences of the United States of America, 104*(46), 17948–17953. Retrieved from https://search.ebscohost.com/login.aspx?direct=true&db=eoah&AN=13211852&site=ehost-live&scope=site&custid=s5099118

Baron-Cohen, S. (1991). *Precursors to a theory of mind: Understanding attention in others*. In A. Whiten (Ed.), *Natural theories of mind: Evolution, development, and simulation of everyday mindreading* (pp. 233–251). Oxford, UK: Blackwell.

Bayne, T. (2013). *Thought: A very short introduction*. Oxford, UK: Oxford University Press.

Beck, J., & Forstmeier, W. (2007). Superstition and belief as inevitable by-products of an adaptive learning strategy [Article]. *Human Nature, 18*(1), 35–46. Retrieved from https://link.springer.com/article/10.1007%2FBF02820845

Bezrukova, K., Spell, C. S., Perry, J. L., & Jehn, K. A. (2016). A meta-analytical integration of over 40 years of research on diversity training evaluation. *Psychological Bulletin, 142*(11), 1227–1274.

Billig, M. (1985). Prejudice, categorization and particularization: From a perceptual to a rhetorical approach. *European Journal of Social Psychology, 15*(1), 79–103. Retrieved from https://doi.org/10.1002/ejsp.2420150107

Bolukbasi, T., Chang, K.-W., Zou, J., Saligrama, V., & Kalai, A. (2016). *Man is to computer programmer as woman is to homemaker? Debiasing word embeddings Fairness, Accountability, and Transparency in Machine Learning*, New York City. Retrieved from https://arxiv.org/pdf/1607.06520v1.pdf

Bothello, J., & Roulet, T. J. (2019). The imposter syndrome, or the misrepresentation of self in academic life. *Journal of Management Studies, 56*(4), 854–861.

Boyer, P. (2001). *Religion explained: The human instincts that fashion gods, spirits and ancestors.* New York, NY: Basic Books.

Boyer, P. (2008). Being human: Religion: Bound to believe? [Article]. *Nature, 455*(7216), 1038–1039. Retrieved from https://doi.org/10.1038/4551038a

Boyer, P., & Petersen, M. B. (2017). Folk-economic beliefs: An evolutionary cognitive model. *Behavioral and Brain Sciences, 41,* e158, Article e158. Retrieved from https://doi.org/10.1017/S0140525X17001960

Brankovic, M. (2019, February). Who believes in esp: Cognitive and motivational determinants of the belief in extra-sensory perception. *Europe's Journal of Psychology, 15*(1), 120–139. Retrieved from https://doi.org/10.5964/ejop.v15i1.1689

Brashier, N. M., Eliseev, E. D., & Marsh, E. J. (2020). An initial accuracy focus prevents illusory truth. *Cognition, 194,* 104054. Retrieved from https://doi.org/10.1016/j.cognition.2019.104054

Brashier, N. M., Umanath, S., Cabeza, R., & Marsh, E. J. (2017). Competing cues: Older adults rely on knowledge in the face of fluency. *Psychology and Aging, 32*(4), 331–337. Retrieved from https://doi.org/10.1037/pag0000156

Bronstein, M. V., Pennycook, G., Bear, A., Rand, D. G., & Cannon, T. D. (2018). Belief in fake news is associated with delusionality, dogmatism, religious fundamentalism, and reduced analytic thinking. *Journal of Applied Research in Memory and Cognition.* Retrieved from https://doi.org/10.1016/j.jarmac.2018.09.005

Bruine de Bruin, W., Parker, A. M., & Fischhoff, B. (2007). Individual differences in adult decision-making competence. *Journal of Personality and Social Psychology, 92*(5), 938–956. Retrieved from https://doi.org/10.1037/0022-3514.92.5.938

Bruneau, E. G., Kteily, N. S., & Urbiola, A. (2019). A collective blame hypocrisy intervention enduringly reduces hostility towards Muslims. *Nature Human Behaviour.* Retrieved from https://doi.org/10.1038/s41562-019-0747-7

Bugnyar, T., Reber, S. A., & Buckner, C. (2016, Feb 2). Ravens attribute visual access to unseen competitors. *Nature Communications, 7,* 10506. Retrieved from https://doi.org/10.1038/ncomms10506

Bullivant, S., Farias, M., Lanman, J., & Lee, L. (2019). *Understanding unbelief: Atheists and agnostics around the world.* Twickenham, UK: St Mary's University.

Buttelmann, D., Carpenter, M., Call, J., & Tomasello, M. (2007, Jul). Enculturated chimpanzees imitate rationally. *Developmental Science, 10*(4), F31–F38. Retrieved from https://doi.org/10.1111/j.1467-7687.2007.00630.x

Call, J., & Tomasello, M. (2008, May). Does the chimpanzee have a theory of mind? 30 years later. *Trends in Cognitive Sciences, 12*(5), 187–192. Retrieved from https://doi.org/10.1016/j.tics.2008.02.010

Case, R. (1985). *Intellectual development: Birth to Adulthood.* New York, NY: Academic Press.

Chan, M. S., Jones, C. R., Jamieson, K. H., & Albarracin, D. (2017, Nov). Debunking: A meta-analysis of the psychological efficacy of messages countering misinformation. *Psychological Science, 28*(11), 1531–1546. Retrieved from https://doi.org/10.1177/0956797617714579

Charness, N., Krampe, R., & Mayr, U. (1996). The role of practice and coaching in entrepreneurial skill domains: An international comparison of life-span chess skill acquisition. In K. A. Ericsson (Ed.), *The road to excellence: The acquisition of expert performance in the arts and sciences, sports and games.* Hillsdale, NJ: Erlbaum.

Chase, W. G., & Simon, H. A. (1973). Perception in chess. *Cognitive Psychology, 4*, 55–81.

Chater, N. (2018). *The mind is flat.* London, UK: Allen Lane.

Cheng, P. W., & Holyoak, K. J. (1985). Pragmatic reasoning schemas. *Cognitive Psychology, 17*(4), 391–416.

Chomsky, N. (1957). *Syntactic structures.* The Hague/Paris: Mouton.

Chomsky, N. (1959). A review of b. F. Skinner's verbal behavior. *Language, 35*(1), 26–58.

Clance, P. R., & O'Toole, M. A. (1987, 1987/12/16). The imposter phenomenon. *Women Therapy, 6*(3), 51–64. Retrieved from https://doi.org/10.1300/J015V06N03_05

Clark, A. (2013, Jun). Whatever next? Predictive brains, situated agents, and the future of cognitive science. *Behavioral and Brain Sciences, 36*(3), 181–204. Retrieved from https://doi.org/10.1017/S0140525X12000477

Conan Doyle, A. (1887/2018). *A study in scarlet.* Hollywood, FL: Simon and Brown.

Conan Doyle, A. (1892/2019). *The blue carbuncle.* London, UK: Daunt Books. (Original publication 1892)

Confer, J. C., Easton, J. A., Fleischman, D. S., Goetz, C. D., Lewis, D. M. G., Perilloux, C., & Buss, D. M. (2010). Evolutionary psychology: Controversies, questions, prospects, and limitations. *American Psychologist, 65*(2), 110–126. Retrieved from https://doi.org/10.1037/a0018413

Cook, J., & Lewandowsky, S. (2016). Rational irrationality: Modeling climate change belief polarization using Bayesian networks [Article]. *Topics in Cognitive Science, 8*(1), 160–179. Retrieved from https://doi.org/10.1111/tops.12186

Corr, P., & Plagnol, A. (2019). *Behavioral economics: The basics.* London, UK: Routledge.

Cosmides, L., & Tooby, J. (1992). Cognitive adaptations for social exchange. In J. Barkow, L. Cosmides, & J. Tooby (Eds.), *The adapted mind.* Oxford, UK: Oxford University Press.

Cosmides, L., & Tooby, J. (2011). Evolutionary psychology: A primer. Retrieved 20 Aug 2019, from www.psych.ucsb.edu/research/cep/primer.html.

Cossins, D. (2018). *Discriminating algorithms: 5 times AI showed prejudice. New Scientist.* Retrieved 2 May 2019, from https://www.newscientist.com/article/2166207-discriminating-algorithms-5-times-ai-showed-prejudice/

Damisch, L., Stoberock, B., & Mussweiler, T. (2010). Keep your fingers crossed! How superstition improves performance [Article]. *Psychological Science, 21*(7), 1014–1020. Retrieved from https://doi.org/10.1177/0956797610372631

Danner, F. N., & Day, M. C. (1977). Eliciting formal operations. *Child Development, 48,* 1600–1606.

Darke, P. R., & Freedman, J. L. (1997). The belief in good luck scale. *Journal of Research in Personality, 31,* 486–511.

Dawkins, R. (1976). *The selfish gene.* Oxford, UK: Oxford University Press.

De Groot, A. D. (1965). *Thought and choice in chess.* The Hague: Mouton.

De keersmaecker, J., & Roets, A. (2017). 'Fake news': Incorrect, but hard to correct. The role of cognitive ability on the impact of false information on social impressions. *Intelligence, 65,* 107–110. Retrieved from https://doi.org/10.1016/j.intell.2017.10.005

Dehaene, S., Pegado, F., Braga, L. W., Ventura, P., Filho, G. N., & Jobert, A. (2010). How learning to read changes the cortical networks for vision and language. *Science, 330*(6009), 1359–1364. Retrieved from https://doi.org/10.1126/science.1194140

Descartes, R. (1637/1998). *Discourse on the method: Discourse on the method for conducting one's reason well and for seeking truth in the sciences* (D. A. Cress, Trans.). Indianapolis, IN: Hackett. (Original work published 1637).

Deutsch, D. (1997). The fabric of reality. London, UK: Penguin.

Devine, P. G. (1989). Stereotypes and prejudice: Their automatic and controlled components. *Journal of Personality and Social Psychology, 56*(1), 5–18.

Devine, P. G., Forscher, P. S., Austin, A. J., & Cox, W. T. (2012, Nov). Long-term reduction in implicit race bias: A prejudice habit-breaking intervention. *Journal of Experimental Social Psychology*, *48*(6), 1267–1278. Retrieved from https://doi.org/10.1016/j.jesp.2012.06.003

Donaldson, M. (1978). *Children's minds*. Glasgow, UK: Fontana/Open Books.

Eco, Umberto (1990). *The limits of interpretation*. Indianapolis, IN: Indiana University Press.

Elqayam, S., & Evans, J. S. B. T. (2013). Rationality in the new paradigm: Strict versus soft Bayesian approaches [Article]. *Thinking Reasoning*, *19*(3/4), 453–470. Retrieved from https://doi.org/10.1080/13546783.2013.834268

Elqayam, S., & Over, D. E. (2013). New paradigm psychology of reasoning: An introduction to the special issue edited by Elqayam, Bonnefon, and Over [Article]. *Thinking Reasoning*, *19*(3/4), 249–265. Retrieved from https://doi.org/10.1080/13546783.2013.841591

Epley, N., & Gilovich, T. (2006). The anchoring and adjustment heuristic: Why adjustments are insufficient. *Psychological Science*, *17*(4), 311–318.

Epley, N., & Gilovich, T. (2016). The mechanics of motivated reasoning. *Journal of Economic Perspectives*, *30*(3), 133–140. Retrieved from https://doi.org/10.1257/jep.30.3.133

Erisen, C., Lodge, M., & Taber, C. S. (2014). Affective contagion in effortful political thinking. *Political Psychology*, *35*(2), 187–206. Retrieved from https://doi.org/10.1111/j.1467-9221.2012.00937.x

Evans, J. S. B. T. (2002). Logic and human reasoning: An assessment of the deduction paradigm. *Psychological Bulletin*, *128*, 978–996.

Evans, J. S. B. T. (2008). Dual-processing accounts of reasoning, judgment, and social cognition. *Annual Review of Psychology*, *59*, 255–278. Retrieved from https://doi.org/10.1146/annurev.psych.59.103006.093629

Evans, J. S. B. T. (2010). Intuition and reasoning: A dual-process perspective. *Psychological Inquiry*, *21*, 313–326. Retrieved from https://doi.org/10.1080/1047840X.2010.521057

Evans, J. S. B. T. (2017). *Thinking and reasoning: A very short introduction*. Oxford, UK: Oxford University Press.

Evans, J. S. B. T., & Stanovich, K. E. (2013). Dual-process theories of higher cognition: Advancing the debate [Article]. *Perspectives on Psychological Science*, *8*(3), 223–241. Retrieved from https://doi.org/10.1177/1745691612460685

Festinger, L. (1957). *A theory of cognitive dissonance* (Vol. 107). Stanford, CA: Stanford University Press.

Festinger, L., & Carlsmith, J. M. (1959). Cognitive consequences of forced compliance. *Journal of Abnormal and Social Psychology*, *58*, 203–210.

Festinger, L., Rieckon, H. W., & Schachter, S. (1956/2008). *When prophecy fails: A social and psychological study of a modern group that predicted the destruction of the world.* London, UK: Pinter and Martin. (Original publication 1956).

Field, D. (1987). A review of preschool conservation training: An analysis of analyses. *Developmental Review, 7,* 210–251.

Fiske, S. T., & Taylor, S. E. (1991). *Social cognition* (2nd ed.). New York, NY: McGraw-Hill. (1984).

Flynn, D. J., Nyhan, B., & Reifler, J. (2017). The nature and origins of misperceptions: Understanding false and unsupported beliefs about politics. *Political Psychology, 38,* 127–150. Retrieved from https://doi.org/10.1111/pops.12394

Fraser, J. (1922/2002). *The golden bough: A study in religion and magic.* Mineola, NY: Dover Publications, Inc. (Original publication 1922)

Frederick, S. (2005). Cognitive reflection and decision making. *Journal of Economic Perspectives, 19*(4), 25–42. Retrieved from https://search.ebscohost.com/login.aspx?direct=true&db=eoah&AN=8217838&site=ehost-live&scope=site&custid=s5099118

Freud, S. (1954). *Interpretation of dreams* (Vol. Original German work published 1900). London, UK: Allen and Unwin.

Gallup. (2005). Three in four Americans believe in paranormal: Little change from similar results in 2001. Retrieved from http://www.gallup.com/poll/16915/Three-Four-Americans-Believe-Paranormal.aspx

Geary, D. C. (2005). *The origin of mind: Evolution of brain, cognition, and general intelligence.* Washington, DC: American Psychological Association.

Geary, D. C. (2015). *Evolution of Vulnerability: Implications for sex differences in health and development.* Washington, DC: Academic Press.

Gellner, E. (1985). *Relativism and Thinking, fast and slow the social sciences.* Cambridge, UK: Cambridge University Press.

Gentner, D., & Colhoun, J. (2010). Analogical processes in human thinking and learning. In B. M. Glatzeder (Ed.), *Towards a theory of thinking* (pp. 35–48). Springer-Verlag. Retrieved from https://doi.org/10.1007/978-3-642-03|29-8-3

Gentner, D., & Jee, B. D. (2010). De l'alchimie aux sciences modernes: Du bon usage de la pensée analogique. *Sciences Humaines, 215,* 40–43.

Gentner, D., & Jeziorski, M. (1989). Historical shifts in the use of analogy in science. In B. Gholson, W. R. J. Shadish, R. A. Neimeyer, & A. C. Houts (Eds.), *Psychology of science: Contributions to metascience* (pp. 296–325). Cambridge University Press.

Gentner, D., & Jeziorski, M. (1993). The shift from metaphor to analogy in western science. In A. Ortony (Ed.), *Metaphor and thought* (2nd ed., pp. 447–480). Cambridge University Press.

Gentner, D., & Toupin, C. (1986). Systematicity and surface similarity in the development of analogy. *Cognitive Science*, *10*, 277–300. Retrieved from https://doi.org/10.1207/s15516709cog1003_2

Gigerenzer, G. (2014). *Risk savvy: How to make good decisions*. London, UK: Penguin.

Gigerenzer, G., & Brighton, H. (2009, Jan). Homo heuristicus: Why biased minds make better inferences. *Topics in Cognitive Science*, *1*(1), 107–143. Retrieved from https://doi.org/10.1111/j.1756-8765.2008.01006.x

Gigerenzer, G., & Hoffrage, U. (1995). How to improve Bayesian reasoning without instruction: Frequency formats. *Psychological Review*, *102*(4), 684–704.

Gigerenzer, G., & Todd, P. M. (1999). Fast and frugal heuristics: The adaptive toolbox. In G. Gigerenzer & P. M. Todd (Eds.), *Simple heuristics that make us smart* (pp. 3–34). Oxford, UK: Oxford University Press.

Gigerenzer, G., Todd, P. M., & the ABC Research Group (Eds.). (1999). *Simple heuristics that make us smart*. Oxford, UK: Oxford University Press.

Gipson, M. H., Abraham, M. R., & Renner, J. W. (1989). Relationships between formal-operational thought and conceptual difficulties in genetics problem solving. *Journal of Research in Science Teaching*, *26*(9), 811–821.

Gobet, F. (2016). *Understanding expertise: A multi-disciplinary approach*. London, UK: Palgrave.

Gobet, F., & Simon, H. A. (1996). Recall of random and distorted chess positions: Implications for the theory of expertise. *Memory and Cognition*, *24*(4), 493–503.

Godden, D., & Baddeley, A. D. (1975). Context-dependent memory in two natural environments: On land and under water. *British Journal of Psychology*, *66*, 325–331.

Gray, S., & Gallo, D. (2016). Paranormal psychic believers and skeptics: A large-scale test of the cognitive differences hypothesis [Article]. *Memory Cognition*, *44*(2), 242–261. Retrieved from https://doi.org/10.3758/s13421-015-0563-x

Green, L., & Myerson, J. (2004). A discounting framework for choice with delayed and probabilistic rewards. *Psychological Bulletin*, *130*(5), 769–792. Retrieved from https://doi.org/10.1037/0033-2909.130.5.769

Greenwald, A. G., McGhee, D. E., & Schwartz, J. L. K. (1998). Measuring individual differences in implicit cognition: The implicit association test. *Journal of Personality and Social Psychology*, *74*(6), 1464–1480. Retrieved from https://doi.org/00223514/98/

Guilford, J. P. (1950). Creativity. *American Psychologist, 5*(9), 444–454.

Halford, G. S. (1982). *The development of thought.* Hillsdale, NJ: Erlbaum.

Halford, G. S. (1993). *Children's understanding: The development of mental models.* Hillsdale, NJ: Erlbaum.

Hamby, A., Ecker, U. & Brinberg, D. (2019). How stories in memory perpetuate the continued influence of false information. *Journal of Consumer Psychology.* Retrieved from https://doi.org/10.1002/jcpy.1135

Hao, K. (2019a). *Ai's white guy problem isn't going away. MIT Technology Review.* Retrieved from technologyreview.com/s/613320/ais-white-guy-problem-isnt-going-away/

Hao, K. (2019b). *This is how AI bias really happens—and why it's so hard to fix. MIT Technology Review.* Retrieved from https://www.technologyreview.com/2019/02/04/137602/this-is-how-ai-bias-really-happens-and-why-its-so-hard-to-fix/

Harris, R. J., Teske, R. R., & Ginns, M. J. (1975). Memory for pragmatic implications from courtroom testimony. *Bulletin of the Psychonomic Society, 6*(5), 494–496.

Hasher, L., Goldstein, D., & Toppino, T. (1977). Frequency and the conference of referential validity. *Journal of Verbal Learning and Verbal Behavior, 16*, 107–112.

Hayes, J. R., & Simon, H. A. (1977). Psychological differences among problem isomorphs. In N. J. Castellan, D. B. Pisoni, & G. R. Potts (Eds.), *Cognitive theory* (pp. 21–41). Hillsdale, NJ: Erlbaum.

Hayhoe, K., & Schwartz, J. (2017, October 2017). The roots of science denial. *Scientific American, 317 (Return to Reason: the Science of Thought)*(4), 66–68.

Hecht, H., & Bertamini, M. (2000). Understanding projectile acceleration. *Journal of Experimental Psychology: Human Perception and Performance, 26*(2), 730–746. Retrieved from https://doi.org/10.1037/0096-1523.26.2.730

Helmuth, L. (2013). *The disturbing, shameful history of childbirth deaths. The Slate Group.* Retrieved 23 Jan 2020 from https://slate.com/technology/2013/09/death-in-childbirth-doctors-increased-maternal-mortality-in-the-20th-century-are-midwives-better.html)

Heyes, C. (2003). Four routes of cognitive evolution. *Psychological Review, 110*(4), 713–727.

Heyes, C. (2012). New thinking: The evolution of human cognition [Article]. *Philosophical Transactions of the Royal Society B: Biological Sciences, 367*(1599), 2091–2096. Retrieved from https://doi.org/10.1098/rstb.2012.0111

Hinton, P. (2017a). Implicit stereotypes and the predictive brain: Cognition and culture in "biased" person perception. *Palgrave Communications 3,*

Article number: 17086. Retrieved from http://dx.doi.org/10.1057/palcomms.2017.86

Hinton, P. (2017b). *Stereotypes and the construction of the social world.* London, UK: Routledge.

Hobaiter, C., & Byrne, R. W. (2014, Jul 21). The meanings of chimpanzee gestures. *Current Biology, 24*(14), 1596–1600. Retrieved from https://doi.org/10.1016/j.cub.2014.05.066

Hodgetts, H. M., & Jones, D. M. (2006). Interruption of the Tower of London task: Support for a goal-activation approach. *Journal of Experimental Psychology: General, 135*(1), 103–115. Retrieved from https://doi.org/10.1037/0096-3445.135.1.103

Hutson, M. (2008, 03//Mar/Apr2008). Magical thinking [Article]. *Psychology Today, 41*(2), 88–95. Retrieved from https://search.ebscohost.com/login.aspx?direct=true&db=pbh&AN=30096345&site=eds-live

Inhofe, J. (2012). *The greatest hoax: How the global warming conspiracy threatens your future.* Washington, DC: WND Books.

Ito, T. A., Larsen, J. T., Smith, N. K., & Cacioppo, J. T. (1998). Negative information weighs more heavily on the brain: The negativity bias in evaluative categorizations. *Journal of Personality and Social Psychology, 75*(4), 887–900. Retrieved from https://search.ebscohost.com/login.aspx?direct=true&db=mnh&AN=9825526&site=ehost-live&scope=site&custid=s5099118

Jablonka, E. (2011, 22 August 2011). Experiencing Language In *New thinking: Advances in the study of cognitive evolution.* Oxford University. Retrieved from http://podcasts.ox.ac.uk/experiencing-language

James, W. (1890/1950). *The principles of psychology* (Vol. 1). New York, NY: Dover Publications. (1890).

Johansson, P., Hall, L., Sikström, S., & Olsson, A. (2005). Failure to detect mismatches between intention and outcome in a simple decision task. *Science, 310*(5745), 116–119. Retrieved from https://www.jstor.org/stable/3842875

Johansson, P., Hall, L., Sikstrom, S., Tarning, B., & Lind, A. (2006, Dec). How something can be said about telling more than we can know: On choice blindness and introspection. *Conscious Cogn, 15*(4), 673–692; discussion 693-679. Retrieved from https://doi.org/10.1016/j.concog.2006.09.004

Johnson, M., & Morton, J. (1991). *Biology and cognitive development: The case of face recognition.* Oxford, UK: Blackwell.

Jonassen, D. H., & Hernandez-Serrano, J. (2002). Case-based reasoning and instructional design: Using stories to support problem solving. *Educational Technology Research and Development, 50*(2), 65–77.

Kahan, D. M. (2017, 2017/08/03). 'Ordinary science intelligence': A science-comprehension measure for study of risk and science communication, with notes on evolution and climate change. *Journal of Risk Research*, *20*(8), 995–1016. Retrieved from https://doi.org/10.1080/13669877.2016.1148067

Kahan, D. M., Braman, D., Slovic, P., Gastil, J., & Cohen, G. (2009). Cultural cognition of the risks and benefits of nanotechnology. *Nature Nanotechnology*, *4*, 87–90.

Kahneman, D. (2011). *Thinking, fast and slow*. London, UK: Penguin.

Kahneman, D., & Frederick, S. (2002). Representativeness revisited: Attribute substitution in intuitive judgment. In T. Gilovich, D. Griffin, & D. Kahneman (Eds.), *Heuristics and biases: The psychology of intuitive judgment*. (pp. 49–81). Cambridge University Press. Retrieved from https://doi.org/10.1017/CBO9780511808098.004

Kahneman, D., & Tversky, A. (1973). On the psychology of prediction. *Psychological Review*, *80*, 237–251.

Kanai, R., Feilden, T., Firth, C., & Rees, G. (2011). Political orientations are correlated with brain structure in young adults. *Current Biology*, *21*(8), 677–680. Retrieved from https://doi.org/10.1016/j.cub.2011.03.017

Kaplan, C. A., & Simon, H. A. (1990). In search of insight. *Cognitive Psychology*, *22*(3), 374–419. Retrieved from https://doi.org/http://dx.doi.org/10.1016/0010-0285(90)90008-R

Kaplan, J. T., Gimbel, S. I., & Harris, S. (2016, Dec 23). Neural correlates of maintaining one's political beliefs in the face of counterevidence. *Scientific Reports*, *6*, 39589. Retrieved from https://doi.org/10.1038/srep39589

Kay, M., Matuszek, C., & Munson, S. A. (2015, April 18–23, 2015). Unequal representation and gender stereotypes in image search results for occupations. CHI '15 Proceedings of the 33rd Annual ACM Conference on Human Factors in Computing Systems, Seoul, South Korea. Retrieved from https://www.researchgate.net/publication/271196763

Keil, F. C. (2006). Explanation and understanding. *Annual Review of Psychology*, *57*, 227–254. Retrieved from https://doi.org/10.1146/annurev.psych.57.102904.190100

Keinan, G. (1994). Effects of stress and tolerance of ambiguity in magical thinking. *Journal of Personality and Social Psychology*, *67*(1), 48–55.

Keinan, G. (2002). The effects of stress and desire for control on superstitious behavior. *Personality & Social Psychology Bulletin*, *28*(1), 102–108. Retrieved from https://doi.org/10.1177/0146167202281009

Kelemen, D. (2004, 2004/05/01). Are children "intuitive theists"?: Reasoning about purpose and design in nature. *Psychological Science*,

15(5), 295–301. Retrieved from https://doi.org/10.1111/j.0956-7976. 2004.00672.x

Kempton, W. (1986). Two theories of home heat control. *Cognitive Science, 10*(1), 75–90.

Kolodner, J. (1993). *Case-based reasoning.* San Mateo, CA: Morgan Kaufmann.

Kozhevnikov, M., & Hegarty, M. (2001). Impetus beliefs as default heuristics: Dissociation between explicit and implicit knowledge about motion. *Psychonomic Bulletin & Review, 8*, 439–453. Retrieved from https://doi.org/10.3758/BF03196179

Kruger, J., & Dunning, D. (1999). Unskilled and unaware of it: How difficulties in recognizing one's own incompetence lead to inflated self-assessments. *Journal of Personality and Social Psychology, 77*(6), 1121–1134. Retrieved from https://doi.org/10.1037/0022-3514.77.6.1121

Kuklinski, J. H., Quirk, P. J., Jerit, J., Schweider, D., & Rich, R. F. (2000). Misinformation and the currency of democratic citizenship. *The Journal of Politics, 62*(3), 790–816.

Lai, C. K., Marini, M., Lehr, S. A., Cerruti, C., Shin, J. E., Joy-Gaba, J. A., Ho, A. K., Teachman, B. A., Wojcik, S. P., Koleva, S. P., Frazier, R. S., Heiphetz, L., Chen, E. E., Turner, R. N., Haidt, J., Kesebir, S., Hawkins, C. B., Schaefer, H. S., Rubichi, S., Sartori, G., Dial, C. M., Sriram, N., Banaji, M. R., & Nosek, B. A. (2014, Aug). Reducing implicit racial preferences: I. A comparative investigation of 17 interventions. *Journal of Experimental Psychology: General, 143*(4), 1765–1785. Retrieved from https://doi.org/10.1037/a0036260

Lai, C. K., Skinner, A. L., Cooley, E., Murrar, S., Brauer, M., Devos, T., Calanchini, J., Xiao, Y. J., Pedram, C., Marshburn, C. K., Simon, S., Blanchar, J. C., Joy-Gaba, J. A., Conway, J., Redford, L., Klein, R. A., Roussos, G., Schellhaas, F. M. H., Burns, M., Hu, X., McLean, M. C., Axt, J. R., Asgari, S., Schmidt, K., Rubinstein, R., Marini, M., Rubichi, S., Shin, J.-E. L., & Nosek, B. A. (2016). Reducing implicit racial preferences: Ii intervention effectiveness across time. *Journal of Experimental Psychology: General, 145*(8), 1001–1016. Retrieved from https://doi.org/10.1037/xge0000179

Larson, J., Mattu, S., Kirchner, L., & Angwin, J. (2016). How we analyzed the compas recidivism algorithm. *ProPublica.* Retrieved 2 May 2019, from https://www.propublica.org/article/how-we-analyzed-the-compas-recidivism-algorithm

Latané, B., & Darley, J. M. (1970). *The unresponsive bystander: Why doesn't he help?* New York, NY: Appleton-Century-Crofts.

Lerner, M., & Simmons, C. H. (1966). Observer's reaction to the 'innocent victim': Compassion or rejection? *Journal of Personality and Social Psychology*, *(2)*, 203–210. Retrieved from https://doi.org/10.1037/h0023562

Levin, I. P., & Gaeth, G. J. (1988). How consumers are affected by the framing of attribute information before and after consuming the product. *Journal of Consumer Research*, *15*(3), 374–378. Retrieved from https://doi.org/10.1086/209174

Lewandowsky, S., & Oberauer, K. (2016). Motivated rejection of science [Article]. *Current Directions in Psychological Science*, *25*(4), 217–222. Retrieved from https://doi.org/10.1177/0963721416654436

Lewandowsky, S., Oberauer, K., & Gignac, G. E. (2013). NASA faked the moon landing—therefore, (climate) science is a hoax: An anatomy of the motivated rejection of science [Article]. *Psychological Science*, *24*(5), 622–633. Retrieved from https://doi.org/10.1177/0956797612457686

Logan, R. W., & McClung, C. A. (2019, 2019/01/01). Rhythms of life: Circadian disruption and brain disorders across the lifespan. *Nature Reviews Neuroscience*, *20*(1), 49–65. Retrieved from https://doi.org/10.1038/s41583-018-0088-y

Lombrozo, T. (2012). Explanation and abductive inference. In K. J. Holyoak & R. G. Morrison (Eds.). *The Oxford handbook of thinking and reasoning.* Oxford, UK: Oxford University Press.

Lombrozo, T., Vasilyeva, N. (2017). Causal explanation. In M. Waldmann (Ed.), *Oxford handbook of causal reasoning* (pp. 415–432). Oxford, UK: Oxford University Press.

Lubart, T., & Mouchiraud, C. (2003). Creativity: A source of difficulty in problem solving. In J. E. Davidson & R. J. Sternberg (Eds.), *The psychology of problem solving* (pp. 127–148). Cambridge University Press.

Lynch, K. (2016). Willful ignorance and self-deception [Article]. *Philosophical Studies*, *173*(2), 505–523. Retrieved from https://doi.org/10.1007/s11098-015-0504-3

Maier, N. R. F. (1931). Reasoning in humans ii: The solution of a problem and its appearance in consciousness. *Journal of Comparative Psychology*, *12*, 181–194.

Manktelow, K. (2012). *Thinking and reasoning.* London, UK: Routledge.

Marr, D. (1982). *Vision.* New York, NY: W. H. Freeman.

Maruna, S., & Mann, R. E. (2006). A fundamental attribution error? Rethinking cognitive distortions. *Legal and Criminological Psychology*, *11*, 155–177. Retrieved from https://doi.org/10.1348/135532506X114608

McCloskey, M. (1983). Naive theories of motion. In D. Gentner & A. L. Stevens (Eds.), *Mental models* (pp. 299–324). Hillsdale, NJ: Erlbaum.

McCloskey, M., Caramazza, A., & Green, B. (1980). Curvilinear motion in the absence of external forces: Naive beliefs about the motion of objects. *Science*, *210*, 1139–1141.

McConahay, J. B., Hardee, B. B., & Batts, V. (1981). Has racism declined in America?: It depends on who is asking and what is asked. *Journal of Conflict Resolution*, *25*(4), 563–579. Retrieved from https://doi.org/10.1177/002200278102500401

McGlone, M. S., & Tofighbakhsh, J. (2000). Birds of a feather flock conjointly (?): Rhyme as reason in aphorisms. *Psychological Science*, *11*(5), 424–428. Retrieved from https://doi.org/10.1111/1467-9280.00282

Metcalfe, J. (1986). Premonitions of insight predict impending error. *Journal of Experimental Psychology: Learning, Memory, and Cognition*, *12*(4), 623–634. Retrieved from https://doi.org/10.1037/0278-7393.12.4.623

Metcalfe, J., & Wiebe, D. (1987). Intuition in insight and noninsight problems. *Memory and Cognition*, *15*(3), 238–246.

Meyer, R. (2010). Why we fail to learn from disasters. In E. Michel-Kerjan & P. Slovic (Eds.), *The irrational economist: Making decisions in a dangerous world.* Public Affairs.

Miller, G. A. (1962). *Psychology: The science of mental life.* New York, NY: Harper & Row.

Muller, C. A., Schmitt, K., Barber, A. L., & Huber, L. (2015, Mar 2). Dogs can discriminate emotional expressions of human faces. *Current Biology*, *25*(5), 601–605. Retrieved from https://doi.org/10.1016/j.cub.2014.12.055

Newell, A. (1990). *Unified theories of cognition.* Cambridge, MA: Harvard University Press.

Newell, A., & Simon, H. A. (1972). *Human problem solving.* Englewood Cliffs, NJ: Prentice Hall.

Nisbett, R. E., & Wilson, T. D. (1977). Telling more than we can know: Verbal reports on mental processes. *Psychological Review*, *84*, 231–259.

Noon, M. (2017). Pointless diversity training: Unconscious bias, new racism and agency. *Work, Employment and Society*, *32*(1), 198–209. Retrieved from https://doi.org/10.1177/0950017017719841

Norenzayan, A., & Hansen, I. G. (2006). Belief in supernatural agents in the face of death. *Personality and Social Psychology Bulletin*, *32*(2), 174–187. Retrieved from https://doi.org/10.1177/0146167205280251

Norman, D. (1988). *The psychology of everyday things.* Basic Books.

Nyhan, B., & Reifler, J. (2010). When corrections fail: The persistence of political misperceptions. *Political Behavior*, *32*(2), 303–330.

O'Callaghan, T. (2017). How to tell truth from lies. *New Scientist [online].* Retrieved 11 Feb 2020, from https://www.newscientist.com/article/mg23431191-000-knowledge-how-to-tell-truth-from-lies/

Ohlsson, S. (1992). Information processing explanations of insight and related phenomena. In M. T. Keane & K. J. Gilhooly (Eds.), *Advances in the psychology of thinking* (pp. 1–43). Harvester-Wheatsheaf.

Oreskes, N., & Conway, E. M. (2010). *Merchants of doubt: How a handful of scientists obscured the truth on issues from tobacco smoke to global warming.* Bloomsbury Press.

Patterson, F. G. P., & Matevia, M. L. (2001). Twenty-seven years of Project Koko and Michael. In B. M. F. Galdikas, N. E. Briggs, L. K. Sheeran, G. L. Shapiro, & J. Goodall. (Eds.), *All apes great and small: African apes* (pp. 165–176). Springer.

Payne, K., Niemi, L., & Doris, J. M. (2018). *How to think about "implicit bias". Scientific American.* New York, NY: SCIENTIFIC AMERICAN, a Division of Springer Nature America, Inc. (e-pub date: March 27, 2018). Retrieved from https://www.scientificamerican.com/article/how-to-think-about-implicit-bias/

Pennycook, G., Cheyne, J. A., Seli, P., Koehler, D. J., & Fugelsang, J. A. (2012, Jun). Analytic cognitive style predicts religious and paranormal belief. *Cognition, 123*(3), 335–346. Retrieved from https://doi.org/10.1016/j.cognition.2012.03.003

Peters, E., Joseph, S., Day, S., & Garety, P. (2004). Measuring delusional ideation: The 21-item peters et al delusions inventory (pdi). *Schizophrenia Bulletin, 30*(4), 1005–1022. Retrieved from https://doi.org/10.1093/oxfordjournals.schbul.a007116

Petty, R. E., & Cacioppo, J. T. (1984). The effects of involvement on responses to argument quantity and quality: Central and peripheral routes to persuasion. *Journal of Personality and Social Psychology, 46*(1), 69–81. Retrieved from https://doi.org/10.1037/0022-3514.46.1.69

Piaget, J., & Inhelder, B. (1958). *The growth of logical thinking from childhood to adolescence.* New York, NY: Basic Books.

Piaget, J., & Inhelder, B. (1969). *The psychology of the child* (H. Weaver, Trans.). London, UK: Routledge.

Pinker, S. (2018). *Enlightenment now: The case for reason, science, humanism and progress.* London, UK: Penguin.

Planck, M. (1948). *Scientific autobiography and other papers.* New York, NY: Philosophical Library.

Pratto, F., Sidanius, J., Stallworth, L. M., & Malle, B. F. (1994). Social dominance orientation: A personality variable predicting social and political attitudes. *Journal of Personality and Social Psychology, 67*(4), 741–763.

Putnam, H. (1983). *Realism and reason: Philosophical papers,* (Vol. 3). Cambridge, UK: Cambridge University Press.

Quattrociocchi, W. (2017). Inside the echo chamber. *Scientific American, 316*(4), 60–63. Retrieved from https://doi.org/10.1038/scientificamerican0417-60

Raichle, M. E., & Snyder, A. Z. (2007). A default mode of brain function: A brief history of an evolving idea. *Neuroimage, 37*(4), 1083–1090. Retrieved from https://doi.org/10.1016/j.neuroimage.2007.02.041

Revell, K. M. A., & Stanton, N. A. (2014). Case studies of mental models in home heat control: Searching for feedback, valve, timer and switch theories. *Applied Ergonomics, 45*(3), 363–378. Retrieved from https://doi.org/10.1016/j.apergo.2013.05.001

Robertson, S. I. (2000). Imitative problem solving: Why transfer of learning often fails to occur. *Instructional Science, 28*(4), 263–289. Retrieved from https://doi.org/10.1023/A:1003884601109

Robson, D. (2019, 20 February 2019). How to upgrade your thinking and avoid traps that make you look stupid. *New Scientist, 241*, 30–33.

Russell, B. (1928). *Sceptical essays*. London, UK: George Allen and Unwin.

Sakulku, J. , & Alexander, J. (2011). The impostor phenomenon. *The Journal of Behavioral Science, 6*(1), 75–97. Retrieved from https://doi.org/10.14456/ijbs.2011.6

Schmid, P., & Betsch, C. (2019, 2019/09/01). Effective strategies for rebutting science denialism in public discussions. *Nature Human Behaviour, 3*(9), 931–939. Retrieved from https://doi.org/10.1038/s41562-019-0632-4

Schwartz, L. (2011, 30 April–6 May 2011). 17th-century childbirth: "Exquisite torment and infinite grace". *The Lancet, 377*(9776), 1486–1487.

Searleman, A., & Carter, H. (1988). The effectiveness of different types of pragmatic implications found in commercials to mislead subjects. *Applied Cognitive Psychology, 2*, 265–272.

Sedikides, C., Meek, R., Alicke, M. D., & Taylor, S. (2014, Jun). Behind bars but above the bar: Prisoners consider themselves more prosocial than non-prisoners. *British Journal of Social Psychology, 53*(2), 396–403. Retrieved from https://doi.org/10.1111/bjso.12060

Seymour, R. S., Bosiocic, V., & Snelling, E. P. (2016, Aug). Fossil skulls reveal that blood flow rate to the brain increased faster than brain volume during human evolution. *Royal Society Open Science, 3*(8), 160305. Retrieved from https://doi.org/10.1098/rsos.160305

Simon, H. A. (1956). Rational choice and the structure of the environment. *Psychological Review, 63*, 129–138.

Simon, H. A. (1975). The functional equivalence of problem solving skills. *Cognitive Psychology, 7*, 269–288.

Simon, H. A., & Chase, W. G. (1973). Skill in chess. *American Scientist, 61*, 394–403.

Simon, H. A., & Hayes, J. R. (1976). The understanding process: Problem isomorphs. *Cognitive Psychology*, *8*, 165–190. Retrieved from https://doi.org/10.1016/0010-0285(76)90022-0

Simons, D. J., & Chabris, C. F. (1999). Gorillas in our midst: Sustained inattentional blindness for dynamic events. *Perception*, *28*, 1059–1074.

Simonton, D. K. (2011). Creativity and discovery as blind variation: Campbell's (1960) BSVR model after the half-century mark. *Review of General Psychology*, *15*(2), 158–174. Retrieved from https://doi.org/10.1037/a0022912

Skinner, B. F. (1948). 'Superstition' in the pigeon. *Journal of Experimental Psychology*, *38*(2), 168.

Skinner, B. F. (1988). *About behaviorism*. Random House USA Inc.

Somppi, S., Tornqvist, H., Kujala, M. V., Hanninen, L., Krause, C. M., & Vainio, O. (2016). Dogs evaluate threatening facial expressions by their biological validity–evidence from gazing patterns. *PLoS ONE*, *11*(1), e0143047. Retrieved from https://doi.org/10.1371/journal.pone.0143047

Stanovich, K. E. (1993). Dysrationalia: A new specific learning disability. *Journal of Learning Disabilities*, *26*(8), 501–515.

Stanovich, K. E., & West, R. F. (2000). Individual difference in reasoning: Implications for the rationality debate? *Behavioral and Brain Sciences*, *23*(5), 645–726. Retrieved from https://doi.org/10.1017/s0140525x00003435

Stanovich, K. E., & West, R. F. (2007). Natural myside bias is independent of cognitive ability. *Thinking Reasoning*, *13*(3), 225–247. Retrieved from https://doi.org/10.1080/13546780600780796

Stanovich, K. E., & West, R. F. (2008). On the relative independence of thinking biases and cognitive ability. *Journal of Personality and Social Psychology*, *94*(4), 672–695. Retrieved from https://doi.org/10.1037/0022-3514.94.4.672

Stanovich, K. E., West, R. F., & Toplak, M. E. (2013). Myside bias, rational thinking, and intelligence. *Current Directions in Psychological Science*, *22*(4), 259–264. Retrieved from https://doi.org/10.1177/0963721413480174

Sterman, J. D., & Sweeney, L. B. (2007). Understanding public complacency about climate change: Adults' mental models of climate change violate conservation of matter. *Climatic Change*, *80*(3–4), 213–238. Retrieved from https://doi.org/10.1007/s10584-006-9107-5

Storms, M. D., & Nisbett, R. E. (1970). Insomnia and the attribution process. *Journal of Personality and Social Psychology*, *2*, 319–328.

Strandberg, T., Sivén, D., Hall, L., Johansson, P., & Pärnamets, P. (2018). False beliefs and confabulation can lead to lasting changes in political attitudes. *Journal of Experimental Psychology: General, 147*(9), 1382–1399. Retrieved from https://doi.org/10.1037/xge0000489

Swami, V., Pietschnig, J., Stieger, S., & Voracek, M. (2011). Alien psychology: Associations between extraterrestrial beliefs and paranormal ideation, superstitious beliefs, schizotypy, and the big five personality factors. *Applied Cognitive Psychology, 25*(4), 647–653. Retrieved from https://doi.org/10.1002/acp.1736

Tajfel, H. (1981). *Human groups and social categories—studies in social psychology*. Cambridge, UK: Cambridge University Press.

Taleb, N. N. (2008). *The black swan*. London, UK: Penguin.

Teigen, K. H., & Jensen, T. K. (2011). Unlucky victims or lucky survivors? Spontaneous counterfactual thinking by families exposed to the tsunami disaster. *European Psychologist, 16*, 48–57. Retrieved from https://doi.org/10.1027/1016-9040/a000033

Thagard, P. (1989). Explanatory coherence. *Behavioral and Brain Sciences, 12*(3), 435–467.

Thagard, P. (2014). Can a thermostat have beliefs? *Psychology Today*. Retrieved 12 Nov 2019, from https://www.psychologytoday.com/ca/blog/hot-thought/201402/can-thermostat-have-beliefs

Thornton, S. (1995). *Children solving problems*. London, UK: Harvard University Press.

Toates, F. (2006). A model of the hierarchy of behaviour, cognition, and consciousness [Article]. *Consciousness & Cognition, 15*(1), 75–118. Retrieved from https://doi.org/10.1016/j.concog.2005.04.008

Tobacyk, J. (1983). Death threat, death concerns, and paranormal belief. *Death Education, 7*(2–3), 115–124. Retrieved from https://doi.org/10.1080/07481188308252159

Todorov, A., Mandisodza, A. N., Goren, A., & Hall, C. C. (2005). Inferences of competence from faces predict election outcomes. *Science, 308*(5728), 1623–1626. Retrieved from https://www.jstor.org/stable/3841621

Tooby, J., & Cosmides, L. (2015). The theoretical foundations of evolutionary psychology. In D. M. Buss (Ed.), *The handbook of evolutionary psychology* (2 ed., Vol. 1: Foundations, pp. 3–87). Hoboken, NJ: John Wiley Sons.

Tversky, A., & Kahneman, D. (1971). Belief in the law of small numbers. *Psychological Bulletin, 76*(2), 105–110.

Tversky, A., & Kahneman, D. (1973). Availability: A heuristic for judging frequency and probability. *Cognitive Psychology, 5*(2), 207–232.

Tversky, A., & Kahneman, D. (1974). Judgment under uncertainty: Heuristics and biases. *Science, 185*, 1124–1131.

Tversky, A., & Kahneman, D. (1981). The framing of decisions and the psychology of choice. *Science*, *211*(4481), 453–458.

Tversky, A., & Kahneman, D. (1982). *Judgments of and by representativeness*. Cambridge, UK: Cambridge University Press.

Vail, K., Arndt, J., & Abdollahi, A. (2012). Exploring the existential function of religion and supernatural agent beliefs among Christians, Muslims, atheists, and agnostics. *Personality and Social Psychology Bulletin*, *38*(10), 1288–1300. Retrieved from https://doi.org/10.1177/0146167212449361

Vosoughi, S., Deb, R., & Aral, S. (2018). The spread of true and false news online. *Science*, *359*, 1146–1151. Retrieved from http://science.sciencemag.org/

Wason, P. C. (1960). On the failure to eliminate hypotheses in a conceptual task. *Quarterly Journal of Experimental Psychology*, *12*, 129–140.

Weisberg, R. W. (1986). *Creativity: Genius and other myths*. New York, NY: W. H. Freeman.

Wertheimer, M. (1945). *Productive thinking*. New York, NY: Harper & Row.

White, P. (1980, 01/01/). Theoretical note: Limitations on verbal reports of internal events: A refutation of Nisbett and Wilson and of Bem. *Psychological Review*, *87*(1), 105–112. Retrieved from http://0-search.ebscohost.com.brum.beds.ac.uk/login.aspx?direct=true&db=eric&AN=EJ231271&site=ehost-live&scope=site

White, P. (1987). Causal report accuracy: Retrospect and prospect. *Journal of Experimental Social Psychology*, *23*(4), 311–315. Retrieved from https://doi.org/10.1016/0022-1031(87)90043-6

White, P. A. (2009, Sep). Property transmission: An explanatory account of the role of similarity information in causal inference. *Psychological Bulletin*, *135*(5), 774–793. Retrieved from https://doi.org/10.1037/a0016970

Whitehead, A. (1911/1948). *Introduction to mathematics*. Oxford, UK: Oxford University Press. (Original publication 1911).

Wittenbrink, B., Judd, C. M., & Park, B. (1997). Evidence for racial prejudice at the implicit level and its relationship with questionnaire measures. *Journal of Personality and Social Psychology*, *72*(2), 262–274. https://doi.org/10.1037/0022-3514.72.2.262

INDEX